BOSTON'S
HISTORIC HUB

BOSTON'S
HISTORIC HUB

*A Tour of the Metro Region's
Top National Landmarks*

Patricia Harris and David Lyon

Globe
Pequot

Guilford, Connecticut

To the preservationists, historical societies, and tireless staff and volunteers who keep the lights on and the doors open at Boston's National Historic Landmarks

Globe Pequot

An imprint of Globe Pequot, the trade division of The Rowman & Littlefield Publishing Group, Inc.
4501 Forbes Blvd., Ste. 200
Lanham, MD 20706
www.rowman.com

Distributed by NATIONAL BOOK NETWORK

Copyright © 2021 Patricia Harris & David Lyon

All photos by Patricia Harris & David Lyon

British Library Cataloguing in Publication Information available

Library of Congress Cataloging-in-Publication Data

Names: Harris, Patricia, 1949- author. | Lyon, David, author.
Title: Boston's historic Hub : a tour of the metro region's top National Landmarks / Patricia Harris and David Lyon.
Description: Guilford, Connecticut : Globe Pequot, [2021] | Includes index. | Summary: "Historic Boston includes the most rewarding and easily visited of its National Historic Landmarks"— Provided by publisher.
Identifiers: LCCN 2021012476 (print) | LCCN 2021012477 (ebook) | ISBN 9781493057900 (trade paperback) | ISBN 9781493057917 (epub)
Subjects: LCSH: Boston (Mass.)—Guidebooks. | Historic sites—Massachusetts— Boston—Guidebooks. | Boston (Mass.) —Buildings, structures, etc. —Guidebooks. | Historic buildings—Massachusetts—Boston—Guidebooks. | National Historic Landmarks Program (U.S.)
Classification: LCC F73.18 .H3724 2021 (print) | LCC F73.18 (ebook) | DDC 974.4/61—dc23
LC record available at https://lccn.loc.gov/2021012476
LC ebook record available at https://lccn.loc.gov/2021012477

CONTENTS

MARITIME BOSTON

CAMBRIDGE AND ALLSTON

THE OUTER RING

INTRODUCTION

The fact that Boston's past touches us daily is the most modern thing about the city.

—Benjamin Thompson, 1975

We thought about this quote from architect Benjamin Thompson often as we researched and wrote this book. To our minds, it perfectly captures the dynamic of the living, breathing Boston that continues to evolve right before our eyes. The city relishes its history and its seminal role in the growth of our country. At the same time, Bostonians keep their eyes focused firmly ahead.

Readers will encounter Thompson, who died in 2002, as part of the visionary team that reimagined the city's crumbling food market as a joyful gathering spot for a new and revitalized Boston. By the time Quincy Market was rededicated in 1976, Thompson had already designed one of the region's best modern buildings, the five-story, glass Design Research building in Harvard Square in Cambridge. And, for good measure, he introduced Bostonians to Marimekko and other icons of Scandinavian modernist design.

It just goes to show how seamlessly the past and the present rub up against each other in Boston. That interplay enriches city life, imbuing it with a sense of purpose and possibility. Commuters heading to work on the Green Line ride the first subway line in the United States. If they travel on the Blue Line instead, they might exit at a station underneath the Old State House. When they reach the sidewalk, they probably rarely notice that the former seat of British rule is dwarfed by the skyscrapers of Boston's bustling financial district. Boston simply grew up around some of its most notable historic buildings and public spaces.

Folks still worship in King's Chapel, where condemned prisoners heard their last sermons before they were led to the gallows on Boston Common. Other Bostonians belong to the congregation at Old North Church, where lanterns in the spire helped light the way to the American Revolution. They check out books and search the web at the first free large municipal library in the country and they slurp oysters at the Union Oyster House, the country's oldest restaurant in continuous operation. Never underestimate the appeal of oysters!

All of these sites (except Design Research) are National Historic Landmarks. Given Boston's long history and record of accomplishment, it is really not surprising that the city boasts more National Historic Landmarks per square mile than any

Boston Through the Centuries

The National Historic Landmarks in Boston tell a compelling story of the growth of the city over the centuries. But, of course, they don't exist in isolation. We have included this time line to place the landmarks in a broader context and to give you a fuller picture of Boston's evolution from a Puritan settlement to a thriving multicultural city.

1630: English Puritans, led by Governor John Winthrop, settle Shawmut Peninsula, which had been abandoned by the Massachusett people during the Great Dying (1616–1619).

1636: Harvard University opens as the first institution of higher education in the United States.

1686: First Anglican congregation is established in Boston and opens chapel on corner of Tremont and School streets three years later.

1713: Old State House completed as the seat of British government in Boston.

1716: Boston Light on Little Brewster Island begins to guide mariners into Boston Harbor.

1721: Long Wharf built as main trading dock, reaches full length in 1756.

1730: Old South Meeting House, the largest building in the community, dedicated.

1737: Old North Church completed to serve growing Anglican community.

1742: Faneuil Hall opens as the city's food market and meeting hall.

1754: King's Chapel completed on site of original Anglican house of worship.

1768: British troops land in Boston to maintain order.

1761: Christ Church opens in Harvard Square in Cambridge.

1770: The Boston Massacre, an encounter between colonists and British regulars outside the Old State House, leaves five colonists dead.

1773: Patriots disguised as Native Americans leave Old South Meeting House and dump three shiploads of tea into Boston Harbor, an event memorialized as the Boston Tea Party.

1775: Lanterns in the spire of Old North Church signal British troop movements toward Lexington and Concord.

1775: Battle of Bunker Hill, the first pitched battle of the American Revolution, fought in Charlestown.

1776: British evacuate Boston. Continental Congress in Philadelphia adopts the Declaration of Independence.

1790: *Columbia* returns to Boston as the first American-flagged ship to sail around the world, ushering in an era of trade with the Far East and other national and international ports.

1790s: Development of Beacon Hill as a residential neighborhood begins.

1797: USS *Constitution* launched from Edmund Hartt's Shipyard in the North End.

1798: Massachusetts State House completed.

1800: Charlestown Navy Yard established.

1806: African Meeting House built on Beacon Hill to serve growing Black population.

1822: Boston incorporated as a city.

1826: Quincy Market replaces Faneuil Hall as Boston's principal wholesale and retail food distribution center.

1831: Mount Auburn Cemetery in Cambridge founded as a pioneering garden cemetery.

1832: New England Anti-Slavery Society founded at the African Meeting House on Beacon Hill.

1840s: Irish fleeing the potato famine emigrate to the United States and swell Boston's population.

1848: Boston Public Library founded as the first large free municipal library in the United States.

1850s: Concentration of writers and publishers makes Boston the literary capital of the country.

1850s: Boston begins filling the tidal mudflats of the Back Bay to create a fashionable new neighborhood.

1859: Land in the newly filled Back Bay set aside for the Boston Public Garden.

1861: Massachusetts is the first state to send troops to fight for the Union in the Civil War.

1867: New England Conservatory founded.

1870s: Chinese laborers begin to settle in recently filled land of South Cove.

1872: Arnold Arboretum established.

1876: Museum of Fine Arts, Boston, opens.

1877: Trinity Church on Copley Square consecrated.

1880s: Immigration from Italy begins; many settle in the North End, Boston's oldest continuously occupied neighborhood. Jewish immigrants from Russia and Poland follow in the next few decades, settling in the North End and West End.

1883: Frederick Law Olmsted moves his landscape architecture practice to Brookline to concentrate on Boston's Emerald Necklace.

1895: Boston Public Library building completed on Copley Square.

1897: Tremont Street Subway becomes the first subway line in the United States.

1897: First running of the Boston Marathon is held.

1897: Memorial to Robert Gould Shaw and the Massachusetts 54th, the first all-volunteer Black regiment in the Civil War, dedicated on Boston Common.

1900: Symphony Hall, home of the Boston Symphony Orchestra, hosts inaugural concert.

1903: Harvard Stadium completed as home to Harvard Crimson football team.

1903: Jordan Hall opens at New England Conservatory of Music.

1912: Fenway Park, now the oldest major league baseball park in the country, opens.

1916: Great Migration of southern Blacks to northern urban areas, including Boston, begins.

1917: John F. Kennedy born in Brookline in home that would be dedicated as a National Historic Site in 1969.

1920s: Immigrants from the eastern Mediterranean, followed by Spanish speakers from the Caribbean, begin to remake the face of the South End, Roxbury, and Dorchester.

1958: Freedom Trail laid out to connect sites associated with the American Revolution.

1974: Boston National Historical Park established.

1974: Boston Pops July 4 Fireworks Spectacular launched on Charles River Esplanade.

1976: John Hancock Tower (now called 200 Clarendon Street), the tallest building in New England, dedicated.

1976: Quincy Market rededicated as the anchor of Faneuil Hall Marketplace, an inspiration for festival marketplaces around the country.

2005: Completion of "Big Dig" construction project knits together Boston neighborhoods long separated by an elevated highway.

other major city in the United States. There are fifty-seven sites in Boston alone; add in four sites in adjoining Brookline and nineteen in neighboring Cambridge and the number swells. For this book, we concentrate on fifty of the landmarks that tell rewarding stories of Boston and Bostonians. That's a lot of history in 103 square miles, and it will give you a good idea of what Bostonians cherish and what they feel defines them. The list includes a number of historic homes that provide tantalizing glimpses of domestic life over the centuries. But it is surprisingly diverse. Within these pages you will also find a concrete football stadium, two acoustically acclaimed concert halls, a hospital operating room, a Tiffany-designed church interior, the site of a Transcendentalist community, and one of the country's oldest lighthouses.

The federal government does not bestow the designation of National Historic Landmark lightly. The Secretary of the Interior reserves the honor for places that are considered "exceptional because of their abilities to illustrate United States heritage." That's a pretty tough bar, even in a city as historically rich as Boston.

National Historic Landmarks are often confused with the much longer list of sites on the Registry of National Historic Places, both of which are administered by the National Park Service. For quick comparison, the Registry is a list of "historic places worthy of preservation" that are often most significant to a particular community or state. Nominations are first reviewed by the relevant state historic preservation office and, if appropriate, then passed on to a national review board. The final determination usually takes a couple of months.

Applications for designation as a National Historic Landmark are prepared in conjunction with the National Park Service and are reviewed by experts in relevant fields such as preservation, history, archaeology, and architectural history. The process may take up to five years before the Secretary of the Interior makes the final determination, recognizing sites that "tell important stories related to the history of the nation overall."

Greater Boston's many firsts—from the first public arboretum in North America to the first institution of higher education in the United States—certainly fill the bill. The area also boasts the country's oldest Black church building and oldest independent school of music, not to mention the oldest commissioned warship in the world. There is a lot of history to uncover—and when you need to take a break there will almost certainly be a welcoming cafe or coffee shop nearby.

That's not to say that Boston's history is unblemished. The city is still struggling, for example, with its complicity in the trade in enslaved Africans. But as a living organism, Boston seeks to improve. Boston Common, the country's oldest public park and the green heart of the city, has often been the spot where the struggles to embrace the better angels of our nature come to light. Patriots railed against British tyranny, abolitionists protested slavery, and women marched for the right to vote. In more recent times, supporters have marched and raised banners to support

LGBTQ+ rights, to demand action on climate change, and to assert that Black Lives Matter. Almost four hundred years old, Boston Common is still a place where people gather to air their views and to help write the next chapters of the city's and the nation's story.

Please savor your journey through Boston history.

—Patricia Harris and David Lyon
Cambridge, Massachusetts

BOSTON COMMON

F O U N D E D

1634

CITY OF BOSTON
DEPARTMENT OF PARKS AND RECREATION

MARTIN J. WALSH, MAYOR

DOWNTOWN AND THE MARKETS

Boston Common

Bordered by Tremont, Park, Beacon, Charles, and Boylston streets; friendsofthepublicgarden.org; open year-round; free. T: Park, Boylston

Boston was only four years old when Boston Common was established in 1634. Puritan settlers purchased the land from William Blackstone. The Anglican minister and hermit was the first European to lay claim to the area after the Massachusett tribe had abandoned their settlement during the 1616-19 "Great Dying."

History records that each homeowner chipped in six shillings toward the purchase price of thirty pounds. The Founders Memorial along the Beacon Street edge

of the Common depicts Blackstone welcoming John Winthrop, Governor of the Massachusetts Bay Colony, to the Shawmut Peninsula. Erected in 1930 to mark Boston's tricentennial, the monument also records Winthrop's aspiration that the new town "shall be as a city upon a hill."

It is hard to tell what thirty British pounds might equal in today's currency. But there is no doubt that the savvy settlers got themselves a good deal. The 50-acre park is the oldest in the country and remains the green heart of the city, the place where all its residents and its visitors cross paths.

It is impossible to imagine the history of Boston without Boston Common. Following the English model, the land was originally set aside as a commons to be equally shared by all residents of the community. Its principal use was as a military training field and as pasture for the town's herd of seventy milk cows. Properly speaking, it is "the Common" or "Boston Common," but never "the Boston Common."

Other uses soon intervened. The cattle had to make room for whipping posts, pillories, and stocks to punish those who went against the order of the Puritan leaders. More serious offenders, including murderers, thieves, witches, pirates, and even Quaker religious dissenters, met their deaths by hanging from the so-called "Great Elm" that an 1876 storm finally destroyed.

It was inevitable that the Common would be a stage for events leading up to the Revolution. Patriot Samuel Adams gathered crowds to rail against mistreatment by the British crown. With trouble brewing, British regulars established an encampment on the Common in 1768. At the time, the waters of the Charles River rose to the edge of the Common on the Charles Street side at high tide. That's where the British troops boarded boats to cross the river and begin their march on Lexington and Concord and, two month later, their assault on Bunker Hill (see page 85).

Many of those soldiers rest in perpetuity in the Central Burying Ground on the Boylston Street side. Established in 1756, it was Boston's fourth graveyard. Painter Gilbert Stuart, most famous for his 1796 unfinished portrait of George Washington reproduced on the $1 bill, is also buried here. Entry into the burying ground is through a small gate on Boylston Street near the Tremont Street corner.

Some of Boston's most luxurious mansions were rising on Beacon Hill by the early nineteenth century, making it Boston's most prestigious address. By 1830, cows were no longer welcome as the Common completed its transformation from pasture to park. Crowds delighted at balloon ascensions and early football games, but the Common also turned to the serious business of hosting antislavery protests and Civil War recruitment rallies.

The most moving and artistically accomplished of the Common's sculptures memorializes the 54th Regiment of the Massachusetts Infantry. The first all-volunteer Black regiment in the Union army was led by Colonel Robert Gould Shaw, a member of a wealthy abolitionist family. Shaw and nearly half his men died while leading an assault on Fort Wagner, South Carolina on July 19, 1863. Shaw's family rejected plans for a traditional equestrian statue of the colonel, insisting instead that he be shown with his regiment. Sculptor Augustus Saint-Gaudens summoned the full extent of his powers to capture the moment when Shaw and the line of proud soldiers marched past cheering crowds in front of the State House on their way to war. The memorial, which sits on the Beacon Street edge of the Common, was dedicated on May 30, 1897. It is the ostensible subject of "For the Union Dead," one of Robert Lowell's most famous poems. "At the dedication," Lowell wrote, "William James could almost hear the bronze Negroes breathe."

Just three months after the unveiling, a new era dawned on Boston Common. At 6:02 a.m. on September 1, 1897, the first trolley car rolled down the underground tracks between the Public Garden and Park Street stations. Before the day was out, more than 100,000 people had experienced the ride on America's first subway (see page 6).

Lying at the juncture of the Red and Green lines of the MBTA, the Common has both the expanse and the supporting transportation to serve as the city's soapbox. Protesters have rallied against the Vietnam war, in support of Northern Irish

hunger strikers, in favor of LGBTQ+ rights, and against racial injustice. Members of Occupy Boston gathered supporters to their fight for economic equality. Others have demanded greater action to combat climate change. White nationalists holding a free speech rally were met with double their number of counterprotesters. The Common is the stage where First Amendment rights are exercised to the ragged limits of the United States Constitution.

On April 23, 1965, Reverend Martin Luther King Jr. led a freedom march from Roxbury to Boston Common. "Now is the time to make real the promise of democracy," he told the crowd of 22,000. "Now is the time to make brotherhood a reality. Now is the time." On October 1, 1979, Pope John Paul II celebrated the first papal Mass in North America before a crowd of 400,000.

But the Common also has its lighter side. In summer, children beat the heat at the Frog Pond spray pool. Now paved, it is the last of three ponds surviving from the original landscape. Tennis players take to the courts and folks gather to watch baseball games. More than 50,000 people turn out each summer to watch free Commonwealth Shakespeare Company performances at the 1912 Parkman Bandstand.

In winter, the Frog Pond becomes an ice-skating rink. The province of Nova Scotia sends Boston a towering fir or spruce tree in thanks for the city's relief efforts after the devastating 1917 Halifax explosion. Up to 50 feet tall, the tree is the centerpiece of the holiday light display. Shortly thereafter, fireworks brighten the sky above the Common as the city celebrates New Year's Eve.

In the early twentieth century, the sons of pioneering landscape architect Frederick Law Olmsted (see page 180) helped bring order and consistency to the walking paths and plantings. For those in search of a peaceful respite, there is always a place to spread a blanket on the grass for a picnic, to find a shady bench to read a book, or a sunny bench to eat a hot dog from a street vendor while listening to riffs from a jazz saxophonist playing for change. After nearly four centuries, the spirit of the English commons still holds true. Boston Common is for everyone.

Tremont Street Subway
Park Street and Boylston Street stations, Boston Common; mbta .com; 617-222-3200; fares charged.

Boston's traffic jams are so legendary that they even have their own lexicon. In the 1960s, traffic reporters Joe Green and Kevin O'Keefe began surveying the streets from helicopters and came up with clever descriptions of the scene below. "The snail trail," for example, perfectly encapsulates the painfully slow pace of the morning commute.

But traffic jams are nothing new. By the late nineteenth century, the main downtown thoroughfare of Tremont Street was often a congested knot of electric streetcars and trolleys, horse-drawn trolleys and private carriages, and pedestrians.

To tackle the problem, the Boston Transit Commission was established in 1894. The first such public transportation agency in the country, it looked to Europe for a solution. The commission proposed building a subway system similar to those already in operation in Paris, London, and Glasgow, and under construction in Budapest. Despite resistance from businesses, some prominent citizens, and those generally unenthusiastic about an underground commute, a public referendum to start construction was approved. On March 28, 1895, officials gathered to break ground for the Tremont Street Subway.

To make the construction process as quick and painless as possible, Boston's tunnels were buried only 50 feet belowground. (London's original tunnels, by contrast, were 100–200 feet deep.) Engineers drew on the experiences of London and Paris to devise their own construction technique. Lengths of trenches were dug to about six feet deep, reinforced with wooden braces, and sealed on the surface. Workers could continue to excavate to the specified depth while the street-level roadway remained in use. When excavation was complete, the tunnels were strengthened with steel-reinforced concrete and topped with an arched brick roof.

Boston's method proved so successful that it became the template for nearly all subway construction in the United States. Not everything proceeded according to plan, of course. Less than a month after work began, human remains were unearthed under Boylston Street near the 1756 Central Burying Ground. Ultimately about 910 bodies were reburied and identified by a plaque that reads: "Here were interred the remains of persons found under the Boylston Street Mall during the digging of the Subway, 1895." Construction was almost complete in March 1897 when a spark from a trolley wheel met a leak in a gas line and caused a deadly explosion near the corner of Tremont and Boylston streets. It seemed as if some of the most dire predictions of the subway naysayers were coming to pass.

Yet work proceeded. Finally, on September 1, 1897, Bostonians greeted the opening of the first subway line in the United States with great fanfare and enthusiasm. By the end of the day, more than 100,000 people had taken the roughly half-mile ride between the Public Garden and Park Street stations, passing through the Boylston Street station along the way. By autumn of 1898, the full route from the Public Garden to North Station, with a separate loop to Adams Square (current site of Boston City Hall), was operational. The underground line connected to street-level lines on each end. The contours of Boston's cut-down hills meant laying five miles of track to cover a distance slightly under three miles. The Tremont Street Subway recorded about 50 million passenger rides during its first year of full operation.

The city began expanding the subway system in 1912 and in 1914 closed the Public Garden station. In 1947, a new agency, the Metropolitan Transit Authority, took over subway management. It has since morphed into the Massachusetts Bay Transportation Authority, more commonly known as the MBTA, or simply the T. The original Tremont Street Subway has been folded into the T's Green Line, which averages about 150,000 weekday trips. Passengers still board and exit trains at Park Street and Boylston Street.

The Park Street station has been enlarged, particularly with the addition of the Red Line platform below the Green Line. The Boylston Street station, on the other hand, is little changed. Both stations are easily identified by their granite headhouses with glass roofs. They were designed in the classical revival style by Edward M. Wheelwright, the city's architect from 1891 to 1895.

According to the MBTA, about 20,000 people take rides to or from Park Street every day. The commute is just part of the daily routine for many folks in Greater Boston. They are often so harried and hurried that they barely notice the 110-foot-long mosaic mural, *Celebration of the Underground*, mounted on the wall just across from Green Line Track 1. The late artist, Lilli Ann K. Rosenberg, created it in 1978 to convey the air of excitement that swept the city when the subway was new and was just beginning its journey below the streets of Boston. All the figures (except perhaps the lady trumpeter) are smiling, and there is not a straphanger in sight.

King's Chapel
58 Tremont Street; 617-227-2155; kings-chapel.org; open for visits and tours April through October; donation requested. T: Park Street

King's Chapel has held down the corner of Tremont and School streets since 1689 as the city of Boston has grown around it. It was home to the first Anglican congregation in New England, established in 1686, and the first in Boston that did not adhere to Puritan strictures. Not entirely welcome in what its founders described as Boston's "Puritan stronghold," the worshippers bounced around for several years before the royal governor seized a portion of a city-owned cemetery as a building site. Now called King's Chapel Burying Ground, the 1630 cemetery was the first place where Puritans laid their dead to rest.

Little is known about the wooden chapel that opened in 1689, except that it was soon too small. It was enlarged in 1710 and the first pipe organ in a New England church was installed three years later. By the middle of the century church leaders decided that the growing congregation needed a bigger chapel. Reverend Henry Caner wrote to self-taught architect Peter Harrison in Newport, Rhode Island, noting that the building committee "would esteem it a Favor if you would oblige them with a Draught of a handsome church agreeable to the Limitts hereinafter assigned." Working with specified measurements and referring to architectural engravings and handbooks, Harrison created his design without visiting the site. King's Chapel was only his second building, but demonstrated his clear understanding of the classical restraint and symmetry of the English Georgian style.

Constructed of rough-cut granite quarried in Quincy, the new chapel was completed in 1754 through a unique building process. The congregation continued to gather in the wooden chapel while the stone church rose around it. Finally, the earlier chapel was dismantled and the debris was thrown out the windows to reveal a graceful interior flooded with light from tiers of windows along both side walls and the arched Palladian window on the altar end. Perhaps reflecting the social status of the congregation, the interior featured pairs of massive Corinthian columns with fluted shafts and intricate capitals rather than the more spare single columns typical of major Georgian churches in the colonies. Twin columns marching down the sanctuary to the altar give the church interior a powerful visual rhythm.

The front porch, with its 25-foot Ionic columns, wasn't completed until 1787 and was constructed of wood rather than the stone specified by Harrison. As the crowning touch, the architect had designed an elaborate spire with two stories of columns to top the 26-foot-square stone tower. Due to cost overruns, it was never completed. However, the belfry does hold the largest bell ever cast by the foundry of Paul Revere and Son. The 2,437-pound bell was installed in 1816 and declared by Paul Revere to be "the sweetest sounding."

Everyone knew their place within King's Chapel. The pew opposite the pulpit was reserved for the royal governor, while the wealthy members of the congregation purchased the remaining box pews in the sanctuary and outfitted them to their taste and comfort. Less well-to-do members sat in the rear gallery along with African Americans, both free and enslaved. The least desirable seat in the house must have been the pew to the right of the main entrance. Condemned prisoners made a last stop at King's Chapel to hear a sermon before they were hanged on Boston Common (see page 1).

The Anglican congregation only enjoyed their new chapel for about two decades before the reverend left Boston in 1776. Church members who chose to stay in Boston during the Revolution worshipped instead at Trinity Church (see page 108). The Puritan members of Old South Meeting House (see page 13) worshipped at King's Chapel while the British used their building as a stable.

The congregation returned to King's Chapel in 1782 and expected to become part of the newly formed American Episcopal church. But the Episcopalians declined to ordain James Freeman, the lay reader at King's Chapel who had taken it upon himself to alter the church's liturgy to conform to his own theological thinking and the independent mindset of the remaining members. Specifically, he revised the traditional Anglican Book of Common Prayer to remove prayers to the king and other references with dubious scriptural basis.

In 1787, church members chose Freeman's Unitarian theology over the apostolic Episcopalianism. In keeping with Unitarianism's radical critique of traditional theology, the congregation held a lay ordination and elected Freeman as its minister. The act made King's Chapel the first Unitarian church in the United States. Still worshipping within the framework of Freeman's revised liturgy, the Unitarian-Universalist congregation remains an active Christian church.

Visitors are often surprised to learn that the creamy white interior color scheme wasn't introduced until 1915. During colonial times, the double columns were shades of gray, the pilasters along the wall were pink faux-marble, and the pulpit was peach. In the mid-nineteenth century, Victorian tastes prevailed with terra-cotta walls and red carpet down the center aisle. The pulpit was draped in crimson fabric. Yet some things remain constant. The painted wooden altarpieces on the wall of the chancel were a 1696 gift from King William. The 1717 wooden pulpit is the oldest in continuous use in the United States.

An even more dramatic change took place when a church member donated German-made stained-glass windows to replace the clear glass in the chancel. Although the congregation was divided over introducing stained glass, the windows were unveiled on Christmas Day 1863. All but the central panel of Christ at the Last Supper were removed in 1931. From 1936 to 1986, all the chancel windows were covered with fabric or shutters for what the church describes today as "strictly aesthetic preferences." Shutters still conceal the image of Christ most of the year. The shutters are thrown open once a year as part of the Easter celebration.

Old South Meeting House
310 Washington Street; 617-482-6439; revolutionaryspaces.org; open year-round; admission charged. T: State Street, Government Center, Downtown Crossing

The Freedom Trail is such a fixture in the Boston cityscape that it is hard to believe that a century after the American Revolution one of the key stops was considered more valuable for its land than for the building that helped make history. But it is true that in 1876 things looked grim for Old South Meeting House. The brick structure had survived the Great Boston Fire of 1872 that consumed more than seven hundred and fifty downtown Boston buildings, only to find itself in even graver peril several years later.

By then, Old South and many members of the congregation had relocated to the more fashionable Back Bay. New Old South Church, also a National Historic Landmark, was completed in Copley Square in 1875. The congregation planned to sell their land in downtown Boston for commercial use and allow the highest bidder to demolish their abandoned meetinghouse for scrap. When the building was

auctioned in June 1876, concerned citizens rallied to preserve it in place. "Twenty ladies of Boston" famously pooled their resources to purchase the meetinghouse for almost three times the price it brought at auction. Their action bought time to secure the funds to buy the land. By May 1877, the Old South Association had been formed to act as steward for the historic site which opened as a museum that same year.

Such preservation efforts may seem unremarkable today, but in late nineteenth-century Boston they were unprecedented. As historian Walter Muir Whitehill wrote in his 1959 book *Boston: A Topographical History*, it was "the first instance in Boston where respect for the historical and architectural heritage of the city triumphed over considerations of profit, expediency, laziness and vulgar convenience." The success of the Old South campaign helped to launch the historic preservation movement in Boston and around the country.

Boston would have lost a pivotal piece of its history if those nascent preservationists hadn't prevailed.

The third congregation in Boston, many of them descendants of the original Puritan settlers, was gathered in 1669 and worshipped in a wooden meetinghouse on the corner of Milk and Washington streets. Early parishioners included a young Benjamin Franklin. By the early eighteenth century, the congregation had outgrown its quarters and was clearly thinking big.

Their new red brick meetinghouse rose on the same site and was dedicated on April 26, 1730. It was the largest building in the city. In many ways, it followed the conventions of a traditional meetinghouse, including a side entrance, central aisle, wooden box pews, and high pulpit. But with its square tower topped by a spire and two tiers of clear glass windows, it also acknowledged the Georgian style of Old North Church (see page 74), constructed less than a decade earlier. The austere interior assured that worshippers would not be distracted from the words of the pastor speaking from the prominent pulpit. Phillis Wheatley, an enslaved African who worshipped here, was the first Black poet in America to publish a volume of poetry. Her collection, *Poems on Various Subjects, Religious and Moral,* was published in London in 1773. Wheatley gained her freedom the following year.

By that time, Old South had met its historic destiny as the largest meeting place for patriots chafing against the abuses of British rule. Crowds gathered to speak out against the practice of impressing New England sailors into the British Navy, to decry the seizure of John Hancock's sloop for customs violations, or to mark the anniversaries of the 1770 Boston Massacre (see page 19). Things finally boiled over on the night of December 16, 1773, when more than 5,000 men gathered to protest the tax on tea. Realizing that no compromise with British authorities was possible, Samuel Adams gave the signal that launched the Boston Tea Party. A group of men disguised as Native Americans proceeded to Griffin's Wharf and dumped 342 chests of tea into the harbor—a cargo estimated to be worth $1.5 million today. Adams is said to have declared that "this meeting can do nothing more to save the country." After that, revolution seemed inevitable. As Samuel's cousin John Adams wrote, "the die is cast."

Under the command of General John Burgoyne, the British retaliated by seizing Old South, destroying the interior, and converting it to a riding school for the

king's cavalry. When the British were finally driven out of Boston, Old South was an almost empty shell of a building with no pews or pulpit and only one of its original three galleries. By 1783, however, the interior was restored, and despite some changes during the nineteenth century, it maintains its original modest sensibility.

As a museum, Old South also upholds the spirit of the building and those who gathered there. Programs and exhibits illuminate the struggle to achieve freedom. Old South continues to be a place where free speech is championed as a basic human right. In fact, in 1929, the Old South Association board of directors affirmed that Old South would welcome public discussion "without regard to the unpopularity of any cause." Among the programs presented at Old South, the annual reenactment of the Boston Tea Party in conjunction with the Boston Tea Party Ships & Museum (bostonteapartyship.com) is one of the most highly anticipated.

Old State House

206 Washington Street; 617-720-1713; revolutionaryspaces.org; open year-round; admission charged. T: State Street, Government Center, Downtown Crossing

You could not miss the seat of power in colonial Boston. For starters, the Town House (as the Old State House was then called) squats at the head of King Street (now State Street), where it had a clear view downhill to the main shipping wharf. Moreover, the east facade of the building was adorned with eye-catching statues of the golden lion and silver unicorn, symbols of the British monarchy.

In a too-familiar story of early Boston, the original wooden Town House built on the same site in 1658 had been destroyed by fire in 1711. Its replacement, a two-and-a-half story red brick structure, was completed in 1713 and has proved far more durable. After the exterior walls withstood a 1747 fire, the interior was rebuilt the following year. The Old State House remains the oldest Georgian-style public building still standing in the United States.

The United Kingdom of Great Britain ruled not just Boston but the entire Massachusetts Bay Colony from this outpost, where the royal governor, appointed by the king, conducted business. The colony's highest court and the elected Massachusetts legislature also met here. New laws were proclaimed from a small balcony below the

rampant lion and unicorn. It was here that the ascension of George III to the British throne was announced to his Boston subjects.

It is no surprise that the Town House became a focal point for grievances in the drive toward revolution. George III had reigned for a little more than a year when lawyer James Otis appeared before the court in December 1761 to contest the Writs of Assistance. Otis argued that the writs, which allowed customs officers to search homes and businesses for smuggled goods, were illegal and "placed the liberty of every man in the hands of every petty officer." Despite his eloquent four-hour speech, Otis was ultimately unsuccessful in swaying the British authorities. But his passionate advocacy did help sow the seeds of rebellion. As John Adams later wrote, "Then and there the child Independence was born."

An even more galvanizing event occurred on the snowy evening of March 5, 1770. By then, an occupation force of more than 2,000 British soldiers had been garrisoned in Boston, and tensions were running high between the occupiers and the occupied. When townspeople and Redcoats met on the plaza below the Town House balcony, tempers flared. Many details of the encounter are unclear, but there is no question that five unarmed civilians were killed by British musket fire. The first among them was Crispus Attucks, a former slave of African and Native American descent. Paul Revere, an engraver as well as a silversmith, captured the fray in an

engraving that kept the episode alive as the Boston Massacre in patriots' propaganda. A circular marker of stones set into the pavement in front of the Old State House commemorates the site of the incident.

Attucks and the other victims were honored in a funeral procession and laid to rest at the Granary Burying Ground. But Attucks was not relegated to dusty history. In the nineteenth century, abolitionists pointed to his sacrifice as they made their case to abolish slavery. In his 1964 book *Why We Can't Wait*, Martin Luther King Jr. declared that Attucks "is one of the most important figures in African-American history, not for what he did for his own race, but for what it did for all oppressed people everywhere."

On July 18, 1776, triumphant Bostonians gathered beneath the balcony to hear the first reading of the Declaration of Independence in their city. Following the Revolution, the Town House metamorphosed into the State House for the Commonwealth of Massachusetts, a distinction it enjoyed until the legislature moved to the new Bulfinch-designed State House on Beacon Hill (see page 37) in 1798. During the early years of independence, the British symbols of the lion and unicorn were removed. In 1882, the restoration of the building as a historic landmark restored the symbols. That pair was replaced in 1901 by hammered copper, rather than wooden, figures. Now curious landmarks rather than symbols of oppression, the figures were restored in 2015.

Just as King Street was renamed State Street, the State House was rechristened the Old State House. The remodeled interior served as Boston City Hall from 1830 to 1840. But the former seat of government was mainly rented out to a succession of tenants that included lawyers, saddlers, hairdressers, and even a Masonic Lodge. By the 1870s, the building had fallen into disrepair, and the Boston City Council was ready to have it demolished.

In yet another familiar story, a group of citizens coalesced to save what they considered an irreplaceable piece of Boston history. The newly formed Antiquarian Club was given a major boost when the City of Chicago stepped forward with an offer to move the Old State House west and install it in Lincoln Park. With its revolutionary bona fides on the line, Boston had no choice but to step up to preserve and further restore the building, which was quickly converted to a museum.

Today the Old State House is a bright speck of red brick in a sea of glass skyscrapers and even has a subway stop underground. The museum chronicles the events that precipitated rebellion, revolution, and ultimately, independence. The second-floor Council Chamber has been carefully restored as the command center of the royal governor, while other exhibits and artifacts—from John Hancock's red velvet coat to tea from the Boston Tea Party—represent treasures that echo Boston's place as a leader in the fight to build a new nation.

Faneuil Hall and Quincy Market
Bounded by Atlantic Avenue and Congress, Clinton, and South Market streets. Faneuil Hall 617-242-5642; nps.gov/bost; open year-round; free. Quincy Market 617-523-1300; faneuilhallmarketplace.com; open year-round; free. T: Aquarium/Faneuil Hall, Haymarket, State

Feeding a growing city is no small task. When settlement of the Massachusetts Bay Colony began in 1630, waves lapped the area where the city's early market buildings now stand. The harbor's edge soon developed into a busy market of meat and produce hauled across the peninsula and fish landed at the nearby wharves. As the community grew, the area became so crowded and congested that Peter Faneuil, one of the city's most wealthy merchants, offered to pay for a central marketplace. Some members of the town meeting government feared that a consolidated market might mean higher prices, but Faneuil's proposal squeaked by with a vote of 367 to 360.

Painter John Smibert designed the Georgian-style red brick building. It opened in 1742 with a market on the ground floor, a Great Hall for meetings on the second level, and a grasshopper weathervane on the central cupola modeled after one on

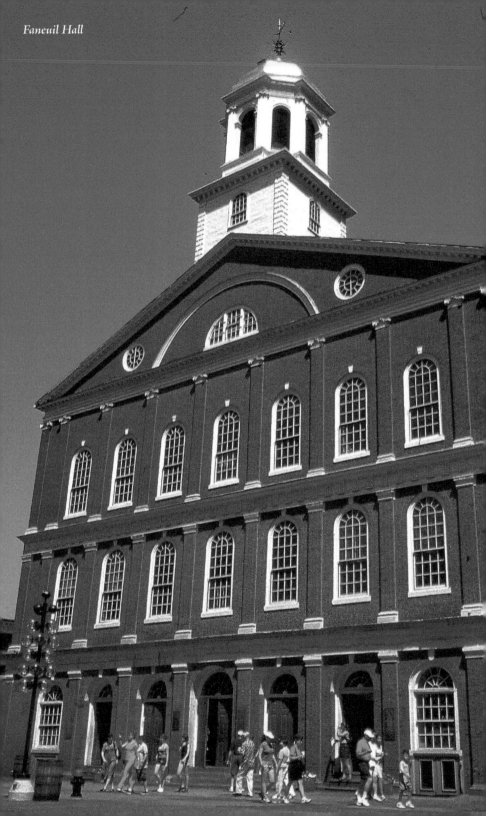
Faneuil Hall

the Royal Exchange in London. In addition to the busy market, it housed the town government and hosted concerts, banquets, and other ceremonies in the Great Hall. The building was severely damaged in a 1761 fire. It was reconstructed and reopened in 1763—just in time for John Hancock, Samuel Adams (whose statue stands out front), and other patriots to lead the increasingly fiery meetings that helped incite the American Revolution and earn Faneuil Hall its nickname as "the cradle of liberty."

The handsome building was named Faneuil Hall after its benefactor. But twenty-first-century Bostonians are reconsidering that name. Peter Faneuil, like some Boston merchants of his era, did not trade solely in sugar, molasses, wine, fish, and timber. He was directly involved in the trade of enslaved people from Africa, and human beings were auctioned off literally steps from the building's front door. That the very emblem of democracy in Boston was constructed with blood money is a stain on Boston history that the city is struggling to properly acknowledge.

Architect Charles Bulfinch oversaw the expansion of Faneuil Hall to triple its original size in 1805 to 1806. But Boston's incorporation as a city in 1822 marked the first step toward moving government functions out of the building. By then, the market was also no longer up to the task of feeding the city. In fact, a Commissioner's Report of the same year described the market area as "a receptacle for every species of filth, and a public nuisance."

Even stripped of some of its original purpose, Faneuil Hall still resonated with Boston's Revolutionary War history. The city retained ownership of the building,

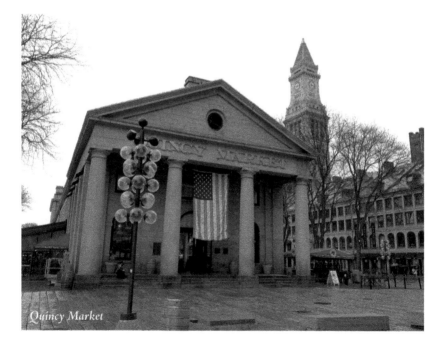

Quincy Market

Quincy Market rotunda

and the Great Hall continued as a storied meeting place. Abolitionists, suffragists, and other reformers have continued to gather crowds to their causes in the Great Hall. Today Faneuil Hall houses the Visitor Center for the Boston National Historical Park, and the Great Hall is a key stop on the Freedom Trail.

Josiah Quincy, the city's second mayor, decided to address the need for a better marketplace with what would be the largest and most ambitious development in the community's first two centuries. Once again, not all of Boston was enthusiastic about

Quincy's plan for a modern market. But eventually he secured $150,000 from the City Council. Before construction could even begin, the city undertook its first major landfill scheme to create seven acres of dry land that would flow from Faneuil Hall down to a new shoreline. A coffer dam was constructed from Long Wharf (see page 133) to the peninsular nub of the North End. The area was pumped dry and laboriously filled by cartloads of stone, rubble, and dirt—most of it trucked in by hand.

Architect Alexander Parris shared Quincy's expansive vision. He designed a complex of three Greek Revival–style buildings that neatly complemented the Federal style of Bulfinch's renovation of Faneuil Hall. Parris's two-story central market house of white granite, modeled on the Greek *agora*, would be flanked by two taller granite and brick buildings to serve as stores and warehouses. (Lots in those buildings were sold by auction.) Parris considered the market house—with columned porticoes at each end and a copper-sheathed dome in the middle—to be the centerpiece of the ensemble. Now called Quincy Market, it remains so to this day.

The cornerstone of Quincy Market was laid on April 27, 1825. Most of the granite was quarried northwest of the city in Chelmsford and Westford and was transported to Boston on barges pulled by horses along the Middlesex Canal. Parris's masterful use of granite resulted in a building that juxtaposed a muscular strength with a sense of bright and airy openness. In contrast to the traditional construction method of laying stone slabs in a horizontal pattern, Parris stood the granite slabs on end to create rows of vertical piers capped with horizontal slabs. Like his Greek

Faneuil Hall

models, such as the Parthenon, the technique created a succession of narrow bays with powerfully vertical windows that flooded the interior with light. Perhaps even more remarkable, the four tapered columns at each end of the building—slightly more than 20 feet tall—were of solid granite, rather than stacked layers of circular stone more common at the time.

Several months after the North and South market buildings had begun doing business, Quincy Market opened on August 26, 1826. It had squeaked in under budget at $149,158.75 and exemplified what came to be known as the Boston Granite Style of architecture. For the next 125 years, the three-building complex served Boston—and soon all of New England—as the central wholesale and retail food distribution center.

But by the mid-twentieth century, the market's raison d'etre was in question. Although many wholesalers still operated in the market buildings, most of the retail merchants had left. They were following the city residents who had moved to the suburbs and begun to shop in shiny new supermarkets. In 1956, the Boston City Planning Board proposed that the derelict buildings be torn down to make way for new construction.

Fortunately, a key group of city officials, historians, architects, and developers recognized that, like Faneuil Hall, Quincy Market and its flanking North and South market buildings also resonated with Boston's history and heritage. Even as Boston leveled other neighborhoods around the markets in the name of urban renewal, the market buildings themselves were spared. Finally, in the 1970s, the stars aligned. Mayor Kevin White, whose vigor is captured midstride in a lively bronze outside Faneuil Hall, fought for a revitalization of the district. City Hall joined forces with architect Benjamin Thompson and the Rouse Company developers to restore and reimagine the markets for a modern Boston.

Work began in November 1975 with the goal of restoring the buildings to their original appearances and creating a district on the model of European marketplaces that Thompson admired. The architect did specify several significant changes to Quincy Market, including the construction of glass canopies along its length. Earlier vendors had often erected awnings to make more room and Thompson's canopies had the same effect of adding space for pushcart vendors and for dining. It was to serve as a tableau for what Thompson called "the sight and smell of food, the cornerstone of human commerce." Elevating the ambience with a dramatic architectural gesture, Thompson had the ceiling of the first floor opened so that visitors could gaze all the way up to the richly decorated interior of the elliptical dome.

Quincy Market was rededicated on August 26, 1976, the 150th anniversary of its original opening. By the end of the day, an estimated 100,000 people had come to grab a bite to eat from the food stalls inside and to share the excitement of a city

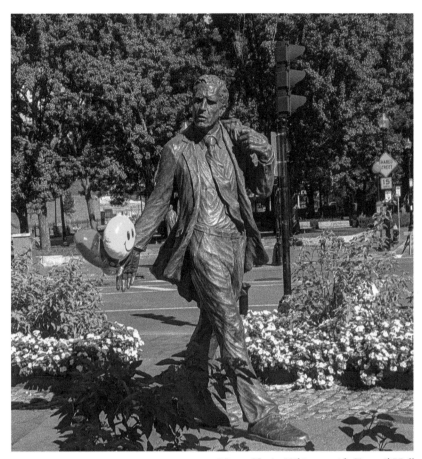

Mayor Kevin White outside Faneuil Hall

shaking off its doldrums. As Benjamin Thompson later reflected, "It was the day the urban renaissance began."

The revitalized South Market reopened a year later and North Market a year after that. The entire complex was christened Faneuil Hall Marketplace to embrace the historic gravitas of the original market building, now the keystone anchor. The project helped create the template for modern "festival marketplaces." The mix of casual dining, distinctive local retailers, pushcart vendors, and street performers—along with lots of outdoor seating and colorful landscaping—was embraced by Boston residents and visitors alike. The Maryland-based Rouse Company used a similar formula to develop Harborplace in Baltimore, South Street Seaport in New York, and Riverwalk in New Orleans.

Over the years, observers have grumbled at the incursion of chain stores while pushcart vendors and street performers have sometimes had a rocky relationship with market management. During much of the year, tourists often outnumber residents. But the market buildings persist, their classical lines suggesting an Athenian heart still beating in the birthplace of American democracy.

Union Oyster House

41 Union Street; 617-227-2750; unionoysterhouse.com; open year-round. T: Haymarket

Sometimes it seems as if every Bostonian has a story about Union Oyster House. Perhaps they once worked there, or a friend did. It is their family's favorite spot for special occasions. Maybe they're history buffs. Or maybe they just love oysters. That craving is, in fact, why Union Oyster House was founded. In the early nineteenth century Americans were oyster crazy. Every city and town worth its salt had at least one oyster bar, because oysters could be packed in moist seaweed in barrels and shipped almost anywhere.

The Atwood family had already opened other oyster bars in Boston, when Atwood's Oyster House—as the Union Oyster House was first known—was

established in 1826. Still in its original location, it occupied a building that was already about a century old on a street that was almost two centuries old. With a few name changes over the years, Union Oyster House is the survivor of the Atwood oyster enterprise. In continuous operation since the doors first opened, Union Oyster House is the oldest restaurant in Boston and is considered by most scholars to be the oldest restaurant in continuous service in the United States. The establishment has expanded over the years and has changed families three times. But the original central section still smacks of the nineteenth century.

That Georgian-style row house near the edge of the harbor witnessed a lot of history. City records show that Hopestill Capen opened a dry goods store specializing in silks and other finery in 1742. *The Massachusetts Spy*, the highly polemical newspaper of the patriot cause, was published on an upper floor from 1771 to 1775. During the American Revolution, the Continental Army paymaster was headquartered here, and women would gather to make bandages and mend clothing for the soldiers. In exile after his own country's revolution, the Duke of Chartres lived on the second floor from 1796 to 1800 and taught French to fashionable Bostonians—before returning to France where he was eventually crowned King Louis Philippe I.

But the building found its best—and most enduring—use as a seafood eatery. Just in from the street, the horseshoe-shaped oak oyster bar still claims pride of place. It is surrounded by nine ancient cast-iron stools bolted to the floor, each featuring a hard, flat wooden seat on top. Oyster eaters barely sit anyway—they tend to lean on the bar with their elbows to avoid dripping juices as they slurp oysters and cherrystone clams from their shells. The shucker presides over the soapstone shucking table (alas, covered in epoxy to meet Boston's health code), digging out the Wellfleets, the Duxburys, the Damariscottas, and more from their piles of crushed ice. Union Oyster House serves about 1.5 million oysters per year and estimates that it takes about 10 seconds to shuck an oyster. That adds up to 4,167 shucker hours per year to satisfy hungry diners—even if they aren't as voracious as Daniel Webster. The orator and politician, who was a regular in the 1840s and 1850s, was said to polish off at least six plates of oysters whenever he stopped in. He washed each plate down with a tumbler of brandy, which perhaps explains his legendary propensity for bombast.

Diners can settle into the original white-painted, stall-style wooden booths, which sit literally two paces farther inside from the oyster bar. Each stall is lined with

The ORIGINAL OYSTER HOUSE

ye olde
UNION
OYSTER
HOUSE
est.1826

LADIES & GENTS

SEA GRILL

UNION GOODS

wooden benches built into the partition walls around a 4-foot-wide wooden table. Louvered half-doors used to be attached at the entrance so that diners could enjoy a little privacy. Movie stars and athletes from Paul Newman and Robert Redford to Larry Bird and Sammy Sosa have found their way to Union Oyster House. As have presidents Calvin Coolidge, Franklin Delano Roosevelt, Bill Clinton, and Barack Obama, who ordered ten chowders to go on Labor Day 2015. John F. Kennedy was more of a regular. When he was in Boston, he would arrive on Sundays at noon to eat lobster stew (alas, now off the menu) and read the newspaper. A plaque denotes his favorite booth, number 18 on the second floor. Every November 22, the restaurant marks the anniversary of the president's assassination by placing a single white rose on the table.

Early menus featured a limited selection of classic New England seafood. In addition to oysters raw or on the half-shell, diners could select stewed, roast, or fried oysters or stewed or fried scallops. Side dishes were simple: bread and butter, fried eggs, extra crackers. Five flavors of pie made up the dessert menu. The current owners have expanded the menu, but they have barely changed the almost 200-year-old recipe for clam chowder.

That continuity in an otherwise changing world is somehow reassuring. In 1931, *New York Herald Tribune* writer Lucius Beebe captured the restaurant's timeless appeal: "The Union Oyster House has been a cathedral, or more properly speaking a chapel, of seafood, its high altar the oyster bar, its acolytes and priests the white-coated experts who render available and edible its Cotuits [a type of oyster] and Little Necks, its worshippers the patrons whose mouths water and whose nostrils quiver at the salt odor of lobster broiling on a coal fire in its kitchens."

BEACON HILL AND THE WEST END

Massachusetts State House

Beacon Hill; 617-727-3676; sec.state.ma.us; open weekdays year-round for guided and self-guided tours; free. T: Park Street

You might say that all roads in Massachusetts lead to the State House. Its golden dome is the marker point for the state's mapmakers and a handy landmark for Bostonians and visitors when they give directions. The city simply would not be the same without the State House overlooking Boston Common from a perch near the summit of Beacon Hill.

But the site was not a sure thing. In the early years of independence, both Plymouth and Worcester vied to be named the capital of the new Commonwealth of Massachusetts, and the legislature also considered building its new capitol in Boston's South End. Finally in 1795, the town purchased the cow pasture that had belonged to John Hancock and settled on the largely untamed and unsettled Beacon Hill as the site for the new State House. A symbol of the aspirations of the new country, it would replace the former seat of British government (see page 19) that had been pressed into service for the fledgling state.

That same year, the legislature gave the go-ahead to a design that Charles Bulfinch had first proposed in 1787. In his early twenties at the time, the Harvard-educated Bulfinch had just returned from a two-year tour of European architecture where he was impressed by the Neoclassical style sweeping through the continent. In drawing up the plans for the State House, Bulfinch was inspired by the Somerset House in London designed by Sir William Chambers in 1775. The stately building overlooking the Thames was, according to Bulfinch, "celebrated all over Europe." Bulfinch's State House would go on to equal acclaim and would influence about half the state capitols in the United States.

Often considered the first American-born professional architect, Bulfinch left a lasting mark on Boston with his designs for public buildings, churches, and residences for the city's most established and influential families. Moreover, his interpretation of Neoclassicism created the template for the Federal architecture that came to define the early years of the new republic. In fact, as architect of the United States Capitol from 1818 to 1829, Bulfinch designed the domed center of the building complex—an echo of his plan for Massachusetts government.

HERE STOOD THE RESIDENCE OF
JOHN HANCOCK:
A PROMINENT AND PATRIOTIC
MERCHANT OF BOSTON, THE FIRST
SIGNER OF THE DECLARATION OF
AMERICAN INDEPENDENCE, AND
FIRST GOVERNOR OF MASSACHUSETTS
UNDER THE STATE CONSTITUTION.

ERECTED 1737.   REMOVED 1863.

Revolutionary War heroes Paul Revere and then-governor Samuel Adams attended the ceremony to lay the cornerstone for the Massachusetts State House on July 4, 1795. By January 1798, the legislature was in session in its new quarters. The building was constructed of red brick from nearby Charlestown and timber from Maine, which didn't separate from Massachusetts and become a state until 1820.

The south, or front, facade of the building faces Boston Common. A paragon of Greco-Roman Neoclassicism, it is designed to impart an air of permanence and gravitas. The central portico juts forth like a determined fighter's jaw. The arcade of seven brick arches on the lower level supports a colonnade of a dozen Corinthian columns on the second tier. Workers carved the columns by hand on the State House lawn, using solid logs 25 feet long and 30 inches in diameter. More than a century and a half later, the columns were replaced with iron reproductions.

Bulfinch left no doubt that the dome, which rests on a central pediment, was a key feature of his design. He called for it to be "inflated to a grand, dominating hemisphere." It is, in fact, 50 feet in diameter and 30 feet high. Originally covered in wooden shingles painted gray, the dome, unfortunately, leaked. In 1802, Paul Revere and Sons returned to cover it with copper sheeting. The dome has gleamed with 23 karat gold leaf since 1874, although it was painted black during World War II to conceal it from view of enemy aircraft. The golden pine cone on the top of the dome is a subtle acknowledgment of the role of the timber industry in building the state.

It took almost a century for state government to outgrow Bulfinch's elegant building. In 1895, a yellow brick extension designed by Charles Brigham was completed.

Grafted onto the rear of the building, it was six times larger than the original but still wasn't enough. Architects William Chapman, Robert Andrew, and R. Clipson Sturgis were called on to enlarge the State House again with white marble wings attached to each side of Bulfinch's facade in 1917. Though greatly overwhelmed by the additions, the power and clarity of Bulfinch's design remains undiminished.

The governor, state representatives, and state senators all go about their business in the State House, which also chronicles Massachusetts history with an impressive art collection. The statues on the lawn—ranging from seventeenth-century religious martyr Mary Dyer to President John F. Kennedy—offer a preview of what is in inside. Visitors no longer enter through Bulfinch's stately front doors. Those doors are opened for visiting heads of state or to receive a Massachusetts regimental flag returning from war. At the end of his or her term, the governor also exits the State House through those doors and proceeds down the steps, a tradition called the "Long Walk."

Bulfinch's doors open onto Doric Hall, which made a grand first impression. Named for the style of the ten columns that lend it an air of ceremonial grace, Doric Hall was used for meetings, receptions, and banquets. The first statue to enter the State House, a marble image of George Washington completed by Sir Francis Chantrey in 1826, occupies a niche in the wall. Doric Hall also features an unusual full-length portrait of Abraham Lincoln painted by Albion Bicknell in 1905. The

6 foot 4 inch president towered over most people and was rarely portrayed at full height. A bronze bust of John Hancock sits between two cannons. Mostly remembered for his exuberant signature on the Declaration of Independence, Hancock was also the first governor of the Commonwealth of Massachusetts.

As somewhat of a corrective to this male-dominated gallery, "HEAR US," an artwork celebrating the contributions of Massachusetts women, was installed outside Doric Hall in 1999. Created by Sheila de Bretteville and Susan Sellers, it honors six women from architect and suffragette Florence Luscomb to educator and pioneer mental health advocate Dorothea Dix.

Directly above Doric Hall and beneath the golden dome, the Senate Chamber occupies the original Bulfinch building. Although it was recently renovated to its late nineteenth-century style, the forty senators still gather beneath a sunburst ceiling designed by Bulfinch. The much larger House of Representatives first met here until moving into a new chamber in the 1895 addition. The elaborate chandelier in the center is topped with the so-called "Holy Mackerel." The dignified chamber's curious piece of whimsy nods to the region's early fishing industry.

But the "Holy Mackerel" is but a fingerling compared to the 4 foot 11 inch "Sacred Cod" that presides over the House of Representatives. In celebration of the fish that made many founding Boston fortunes, a "Sacred Cod" has hung above the legislature since the early eighteenth century. The solid pine codfish, most likely the third, dates from 1784. It was wrapped in an American flag and carried with great ceremony from the Old State House to the new on January 11, 1798.

The 160 members of the House of Representatives sit in a semicircle facing the Speaker's podium and the "Milestones on the Road to Freedom" murals painted by Albert Herter in 1942. One scene depicts John Adams, Samuel Adams, and James Bowdoin in deep concentration as they drafted the Massachusetts Constitution. Adopted in 1780 and amended more than one hundred times since, it was a model for the United States Constitution and remains one of the oldest working constitutions in the world.

Also in the 1895 Brigham addition, more murals grace the marble walls of Nurses' Hall. Robert Reid's early twentieth-century paintings depict Paul Revere sounding the alarm during his midnight ride, James Otis appearing before the British court to contest the Writs of Assistance (see page 20), and the patriots dumping tea into Boston Harbor during the Boston Tea Party. But the room takes its name from another conflict in our nation's history. Sculpted in 1914 and mounted on a marble pedestal, the "Army Nurses' Civil War Memorial" statue depicts an Army nurse comforting a wounded soldier. Although nearly half a century had passed since the conflict, it was the first statue honoring contributions of the women of the Union during the Civil War.

In Memorial Hall on the other side of the central staircase, Edward Simmons's 1902 mural "The Return of the Colors" portrays the December 22, 1865, ceremony when Governor John Andrew received the flags of the Massachusetts regiments that had served in the Civil War. The State House collection of more than four hundred regimental flags from every American conflict since represents the human cost of defending the freedoms and democratic self-rule that the State House itself embodies.

African Meeting House

8 Smith Court, Museum of African American History; 617-720-2991; maah.org; open year-round; admission charged. Black Heritage Trail: 617-742-5415; nps.gov/boaf. T: Park Street, Bowdoin

History sometimes has a wonderful sense of symmetry. In the early nineteenth century, the Reverend Thomas Paul led worship services for members of Boston's African American community in Faneuil Hall (see page 23). Within three decades, the church building that he and his followers constructed had itself gained recognition as the "Black Faneuil Hall."

The Commonwealth of Massachusetts abolished slavery in 1783, but was slower to grant equal rights to its African American residents. They could, for example, worship in established churches but were usually forced into segregated seats in the balconies and denied equal privileges. Some Blacks chose to worship instead in private homes or in public gathering places such as Faneuil Hall.

In August 1805, Paul and about twenty of his followers took matters into their own hands by forming the First African Baptist Church. Both Black and White Bostonians contributed to the $7,700 cost of the meetinghouse. Most of the labor and skilled craftsmanship was carried out by members of the Black community. By December 1806, Paul and his congregation were able to worship in their own African Meeting House. It sat on the north slope of Beacon Hill, almost in the shadow of

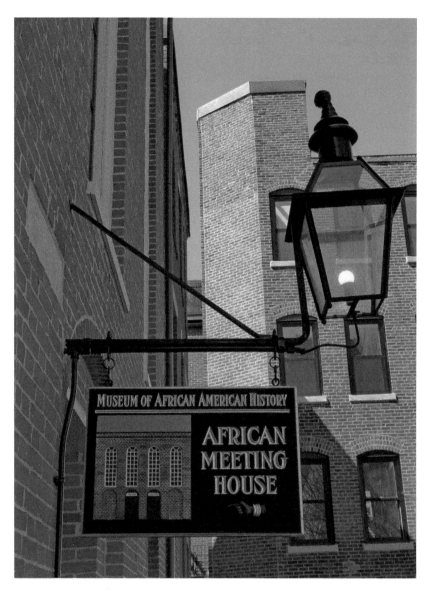

the Massachusetts State House. At the time, about half of Boston's 2,000 free Blacks called this area home.

From an architect's point of view, the meetinghouse fits well into proper Beacon Hill. Its elegant simplicity echoes the neighborhood style developed by architects Charles Bulfinch and Asher Benjamin. Some scholars suggest that Benjamin may have even drawn up the plans, or that some of the Black artisans he had hired to construct the Charles Street Meeting House two years earlier incorporated details from that structure.

The red brick exterior is unadorned, save for four arches at street level (with entrances in the middle two) and four elegant two-story arched windows on the upper level. The interior is flooded with daylight, augmented by brass chandeliers. The ocher pews trimmed with mahogany rails face the pulpit and curve gently like the interior of a clamshell. A balcony, reached by elegantly curving stairs, provides for an overflow crowd.

The Reverend Paul led his congregation until 1829 and was known as a spirited speaker. The meetinghouse quickly became a center of the African American community. They gathered for worship services, community celebrations, lectures, adult education classes, and musical events. Black schoolchildren were educated at the meetinghouse until 1835, when the Abiel Smith School, now part of the Museum of African American History, opened next door. Public schools were not integrated until 1855.

The African Meeting House was the first African American church structure built north of the Mason-Dixon line. It is believed to be the oldest Black church building still standing in the United States. But its most enduring legacy is as the "Black Faneuil Hall," a focal point in the struggle to end slavery and establish equal rights.

Boston's first abolitionist organization, the Massachusetts General Colored Association, gathered at the meetinghouse. In 1832, abolitionist William Lloyd Garrison founded the New England Anti-Slavery Society here. "We have met tonight in this obscure schoolhouse," he proclaimed. "Our numbers few and our influence limited; but mark my prediction, Faneuil Hall shall ere long echo with the principles we have set forth. We shall shake the Nation by their mighty power."

The walls of the meetinghouse also rang with the voices of abolitionists Harriet Tubman, Sojourner Truth, Wendell Phillips, Sarah Grimke, and Frederick Douglass. In her farewell speech, Maria Stewart, a former domestic servant who became a teacher, journalist, and abolitionist, advocated for the rights of both African Americans and women. In 1863, the meetinghouse became the recruiting station for the 54th Regiment of the Massachusetts Infantry. The Shaw Memorial (see page 4), across from the State House, honors the sacrifice of this first volunteer regiment of Black soldiers raised during the Civil War. It is also the starting point of the Black Heritage Trail, which traces the struggles and successes of the African American community on Beacon Hill.

As Boston's African American population grew after the Civil War, many Beacon Hill residents moved to more spacious homes in the South End and Roxbury. In the late nineteenth century, the meetinghouse was purchased by a Hasidic Jewish congregation from the North End for use as a synagogue. In 1972, the Museum of African American History purchased the meetinghouse. With partial funding by the National Park Service, the church was restored to its nineteenth-century heyday. Today, the African Meeting House, once ground zero in the struggle for equal rights, is the final stop on the Black Heritage Trail.

Beacon Hill Walking Tour
Start at Massachusetts State House; free. T: Park Street

As Boston was coming into its own at the end of the eighteenth century, Beacon Hill rose above Boston Common as largely untamed land in the heart of a city beginning to burst at its seams. Eventually, the top was lowered about 60 feet to provide fill for new land from the mudflats along present day Charles Street and the east end of the Back Bay, including what would become the Boston Public Garden.

But Beacon Hill remains the loftiest perch in downtown Boston. You will spend quite a bit of time walking uphill and downhill as you explore this compact neighborhood that has been recognized as a National Historic Landmark for its largely unaltered Federal period domestic architecture.

Twelve Beacon Hill properties have also received individual landmark status. Even apart from their architectural significance, these buildings allude to fascinating stories of their residents and bring to life critical turning points in the social history of Boston and the nation. As you seek them out on this walking tour, you will get a taste of the genteel neighborhood's uneven brick sidewalks, electric streetlights modeled on old-fashioned gaslights, and window boxes bursting with blooming plants in summer. Several of the properties that welcome visitors also have separate, more detailed, entries in this book.

The walking tour begins at the Massachusetts State House (see page 37), which was constructed in 1795 to 1798 on pastureland that had belonged to the family of patriot John Hancock. That official vote of confidence set Beacon Hill on its path to becoming Boston's most fashionable address.

Follow Bowdoin Street along the side of the State House past Ashburton Park, where a re-creation of the Beacon Hill Memorial Column designed by Charles Bulfinch commemorates the "train of events which led to the American Revolution." The column rises to the original height of Beacon Hill before it was cut down to help Boston create new land.

Walk downhill to take the first left onto Derne Street and then turn right onto Hancock Street to continue downhill to number 20, the Charles Sumner House. The fairly modest four-story red brick town house was built in 1805 on the less fashionable north slope of Beacon Hill. Charles Sumner's father purchased the house in 1830 and Charles lived there until 1867—when he wasn't in Washington, D.C. Educated at Harvard and trained as a lawyer, Sumner was elected to the United States Senate in 1851 and served until his death in 1874. A forceful orator, Sumner was an early opponent of slavery. Both before and after the Civil War, his commitment to the cause of "absolute human equality," as the National Park Service puts it, never wavered.

Continue downhill until Hancock Street meets Cambridge Street. Cross Cambridge Street if you want to tour the First Harrison Gray Otis House (see page 59 David Sears House). Charles Bulfinch designed it for one of the civic leaders who led the transformation of Beacon Hill into Boston's most coveted address.

Otherwise, turn left onto Cambridge Street and then left again to climb up Joy Street toward two other buildings associated with the struggle for civil rights. Turn

David Sears House

Harding House

right onto Smith Court, a narrow alleyway that became a focal point for Boston's African American community in the nineteenth century.

At number 3 Smith Court, the three-story Federal-style William C. Nell Residence was built between 1798 and 1800 with a clapboard facade. By the 1830s, it was home to a succession of African Americans and occasionally a safe haven for fugitive slaves. James Scott lived here for almost 50 years and manged to purchase the property in 1865. The building, however, is most associated with Scott's tenant William Cooper Nell who lived here from 1850 to 1857.

Nell was born in Boston in 1816, was educated at the segregated Abiel Smith School at 46 Joy Street (now part of the Museum of African American History), and advocated for civil rights throughout his life. A vocal opponent of slavery, Nell organized meetings, gave lectures, and wrote for abolitionist William Lloyd Garrison's newspaper *The Liberator*. Nell was also one of the leaders in the struggle to integrate Boston public schools. When he became a Boston postal clerk, he was the first African American appointed to a position in the Federal service. A gifted researcher, Nell wrote *The Colored Patriots of the American Revolution* in 1855. It was the first such history published by a Black author.

Almost directly across the street, the African Meeting House (see page 42) played such a vital role in the abolitionist movement that it became known as the "Black Faneuil Hall." Holmes Alley, at the end of the Smith Court cul-de-sac, connects to South Russell Street. Barely wide enough for a human being to pass, it was

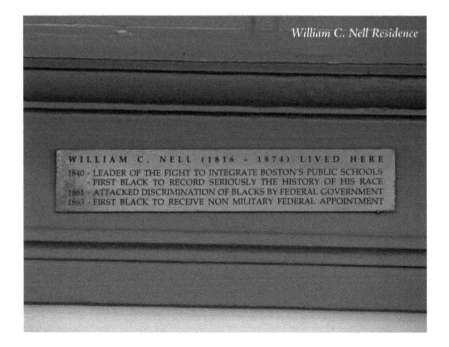

William C. Nell Residence

WILLIAM C. NELL (1816 - 1874) LIVED HERE
1840 - LEADER OF THE FIGHT TO INTEGRATE BOSTON'S PUBLIC SCHOOLS
- FIRST BLACK TO RECORD SERIOUSLY THE HISTORY OF HIS RACE
1861 - ATTACKED DISCRIMINATION OF BLACKS BY FEDERAL GOVERNMENT
1863 - FIRST BLACK TO RECEIVE NON MILITARY FEDERAL APPOINTMENT

part of the network of alleys and neighborhood paths that served to spirit enslaved persons to freedom.

When you are ready to leave Smith Court, retrace your steps and turn right onto Joy Street. You will pass the entrance to the Museum of African American History as you walk uphill. Turn right onto Mount Vernon Street, the broadest thoroughfare of Beacon Hill. Henry James called the stretch of Mount Vernon from the State House to Louisburg Square "the most civilized street in America." If you decide to

Samuel Gridley and Julia Ward Howe House

continue down to the square to see what James was talking about, be sure to double back to turn down Walnut Street and then make a right on Chestnut Street.

The Samuel Gridley and Julia Ward Howe House stands at 13 Chestnut Street. The four-story brick home was the first of three in a row that Hepzibah Swan commissioned from Charles Bulfinch, the architect who defined the Beacon Hill style. Along with Harrison Gray Otis and several other wealthy Bostonians, Swan was one of the chief developers of Beacon Hill real estate. She presented the houses to her three daughters as especially nice wedding presents. In 1806, Christiana Swan and her husband John Turner Sargent moved into their new home at 13 Chestnut Street. The painter John Singer Sargent, whose works in Boston include murals at the Boston Public Library (see page 116), later lived here.

Julia Ward Howe and her husband Samuel Gridley Howe lived at 13 Chestnut Street from 1863 to 1866. The couple were just the type of social reformers that the neighborhood favored. Both were ardent abolitionists and had edited the antislavery newspaper *The Commonwealth*. Samuel, who was trained as a physician, became the first director of the Perkins School for the Blind (formerly the New England Asylum for the Blind), the first such school in the United States. He remained an advocate for persons with disabilities throughout his life. Almost twenty years younger than her husband, the mother of six children was renowned as a suffragist and as an advocate for peace and for educational and professional opportunities for women. While

Charles Sumner House

on a trip to Washington, D.C. shortly after the couple moved to Beacon Hill, Julia wrote *The Battle Hymn of the Republic*, which brought her national fame.

A short walk downhill, number 50 Chestnut Street was designed by architect Cornelius Coolidge, who played a role in developing the south slope of Beacon Hill in the 1820s and 1830s. The Frances Parkman House is named for the widely admired historian who lived here from 1865 to 1893. Born in 1823 to a prominent Boston family, Parkman was educated at Harvard but eschewed a conventional life as a lawyer. A trip across the Great Plains when he was fresh out of school set him on his course as a writer and historian. He chronicled his adventure in *The Oregon Trail*, published in 1849. He devoted much of his life to recounting the struggle between England and France for control of North America. Parkman wrote much of his eight-volume series, *France and England in North America*, in his third-floor study at the front of this house.

At the end of the block, turn left and follow Spruce Street until it meets Beacon Street. With its prime frontage on Boston Common, Beacon Street boasts the grandest houses on the hill. Many of them sit on land once owned by the Colonial-era portrait painter John Singleton Copley.

Turn right to walk downhill to number 55 Beacon Street, one-half of a pair of mirror-image bow-front row houses designed by architect Asher Benjamin in the first decade of the nineteenth century. Less celebrated than his near-contemporary, Charles Bulfinch, Benjamin nonetheless created Beacon Hill homes that rivaled Bulfinch's in their elegance. Benjamin ultimately had a more lasting effect on American domestic architecture through his pattern books that codified Federal and Greek Revival architectural practices.

Following Beacon Hill convention, the home at 55 Beacon Street takes its name from its most famous resident. From 1845 to 1859, the William Hickling Prescott House was home of the historian, who was left nearly blind from an accident while a student at Harvard. A grandson of Colonel William Prescott, a hero of the Battle of Bunker Hill (see page 85), the historian was most fascinated with the Spanish Empire. He chronicled the era in books such as *History of the Conquest of Mexico* and *History of the Conquest of Peru*. The home is owned by the National Society of the Colonial Dames in the Commonwealth of Massachusetts (nscdama.org/william-hickling-prescott-house/), which usually offers tours on Saturday afternoons from June through October. This glimpse of a well-to-do Beacon Hill residence includes Prescott's restored study on the third floor.

As you walk up Beacon Street back toward the State House, you will pass number 45 Beacon Street, the third and largest of the houses that Charles Bulfinch designed for Harrison Gray Otis and his wife Sally. The gracious patrician hosts always left a huge bowl of punch at the stair landing to greet guests.

You won't miss the David Sears House at 42–43 Beacon Street. One of the first houses in Boston built of granite, it features oversized semicircular bays that climb to the roof line. It was designed by architect Alexander Parris for David Sears, a wealthy philanthropist, land developer, and politician. Less than a decade later, Parris's design for Quincy Market (see page 23) would establish him as the master of the Boston Granite Style. The Sears home sits on the site of an earlier home of painter John Singleton Copley.

William Hickling Prescott House

An urban example of the "serial architecture" usually associated with New England farmhouses, the Sears house was built in three stages. The right side rose in 1816, while the matching left side was added in 1824. The third story was added in 1875, the same year that the home was purchased by the Somerset Club. Founded in 1851, the Somerset is considered the most prestigious of Boston's exclusive private clubs, once described by the *Harvard Crimson* as "places where men could smoke the mild cigar and sip a fine brandy while playing cards and catching up on the news from Europe." Under pressure from the city, it began to admit women in the late 1980s.

Alexander Parris was also the architect of the 1817 red brick Nathan Appleton Residence at 39–40 Beacon Street. Like many Beacon Hill homes, it is one of a pair of town houses that mirror each other. From 1821 until 1861 it was the home of Nathan Appleton, a pioneer in the development of the American textile industry. Appleton was the father of eight children by two wives. His first, Maria, died in

Nathan Appleton Residence

Boston Athenaeum

1833. He married his second wife, Harriot, a cousin of Charles Sumner, in 1839. Of his children, he was fondest of his daughter Frances Elizabeth, known as Fanny. Henry Wadsworth Longfellow (see page 163) often climbed the ten steps into the house when he courted Fanny and the couple was married here in 1843. Their happy life together in Cambridge was cut short when Fanny died from burns suffered when her clothing caught fire. Nathan Appleton died on July 14, 1861, the day after Fanny was buried at Mount Auburn Cemetery (see page 168). At the time, he was one of the ten wealthiest men in Boston.

You will pass the State House before you reach the Chester Harding House at 16 Beacon Street. Built in 1808 for real estate developer Thomas Fletcher, the four-story brick building in the Federal style was probably an imposing structure in its day. Subsequent alterations—notably the Greek Revival columns and the second-story bay and porch grafted onto the original spare lines—give the house a vaguely supercilious appearance, especially because it is dwarfed by the flanking office buildings constructed in the early twentieth century.

Its most famous resident was portrait artist Chester Harding. Born in Conway, Massachusetts, in 1792, Harding left school at age twelve. He worked as a cabinet-maker, tavern-keeper, and sign-painter before he found his calling as a portrait

Boston Athenaeum

painter while living in Pittsburgh. Largely self-taught, he did study briefly at the Pennsylvania Academy of Fine Arts. When he first arrived in Boston in 1823, he was in such demand that society portraitist Gilbert Stuart described the desire to sit for the younger painter as "Harding Fever." After several years in London, where he painted aristocrats and members of the royal family, Harding and his family returned to Boston. They lived at 16 Beacon Street from 1826 to 1830 before relocating to Springfield. Following his death in 1866, it was estimated that Harding had completed more than 1,000 portraits. Since 1963, the building has been the headquarters of the Boston Bar Association.

Just a few doors down, the Boston Athenaeum (bostonathenaeum.org) at 10½ Beacon Street was incorporated as a private library in 1807 and was modeled after the Athenaeum and Lyceum in Liverpool, England. Founding members donated both money and books to the fledgling institution. They also quickly built an impressive art collection and established the first major art gallery in Boston in 1827. The Athenaeum supported the establishment of the Museum of Fine Arts and transferred much of its collection to the museum when the latter opened its doors in 1876.

After a succession of short-lived homes, the Athenaeum settled into this catbird seat overlooking the Granary Burying Ground in 1849. Architect Edward Clarke Cabot based the design for the gray sandstone structure on Andrea Palladio's Palazza da Porta Festa in Vicenza, a work he knew from an illustrated folio-sized book on Palladio that was in the library's collection. Nonmembers may purchase day passes or make reservations for guided tours.

First Harrison Gray Otis House
141 Cambridge Street; 617-994-5920; historicnewengland.org; open for guided tours April through November; admission charged. T: Charles Street/MGH, Government Center

Lawyer Harrison Gray Otis and his wife Sally Foster Otis were a young couple on the rise in the heady early years of the new Republic. Their mansion at the foot of Beacon Hill helped launch them on their trajectory.

In the late eighteenth century Bowdoin Square was a peaceful retreat. It was discreetly removed from the congestion of downtown Boston, but handy enough to the seats of business as well as city and state government. Considering it the perfect spot for his growing family, Otis purchased a lot on the corner of Cambridge and Lynde streets in 1793 and commissioned his friend, architect Charles Bulfinch, to design his new home. It was a busy time for the architect, whose design for the Massachusetts State House would begin to rise on the peak of Beacon Hill in 1795 and would ultimately influence the style of about half the state capitols in the country.

But Bulfinch didn't refuse his friend. Instead, he created an elegant mansion with the classical lines and fine detail that literally define Federal period architecture in Boston.

The Otises and four of their children (the couple eventually had eleven) moved into their home in 1796. The front facade of the three-story brick building is a study in symmetry. A fanlight tops the central main entry door. A Palladian window sits above on the second level, and another fanlight on the third. Sets of two windows on each side flank those central elements.

That graceful balance continues inside. As befitted a couple who loved to entertain (and were known as gracious hosts), the entry opens into a wide central hall facing a broad stairway. Two massive rooms on the front of the house spoke to the importance of its owners: a sweeping dining room on the left, and an equally impressive front parlor on the right.

For many years, Otis House curators presented the home in the "Williamsburg Colonial" style of plain, even somber decor. But in the 1970s, careful historic and scientific research revealed that the Otises favored a bright, even flamboyant style that almost always surprises today's visitors. In the front parlor, the fireplace surround and lower portion of the walls are painted a light aqua, a settee is upholstered in bright red, and the wallpaper border features illustrated scenes of ancient Pompeii.

The red drapery and yellow walls in the dining room are offset by the brilliant blue paint that circles the lower walls and continues around the fireplace. For the dining room restoration, curators took some cues from the 1824 painting *The Dinner Party* by Boston artist Henry Sargent. Although the scene most likely depicts Sargent's own Bulfinch-designed town house, it captures the taste of well-to-do Bostonians, down to the fine carpets protected by green "crumb cloths" under the table.

Otis's office at the rear of the house features wallpaper in a bold geometric design and a hidden safe built into the fireplace mantel.

The Otises would also entertain certain guests in the withdrawing room on the second floor, where they might enjoy tea or play games or listen to music. It was the finest room in the house, where some of their prized possessions could shine. The reflective gold brocade-pattern wallpaper would glow in the candlelight. A free-standing harp, a small clavichord, and a gaming table on one end and a fine tea table at the other evoke the period amusements.

Across the central hall, Sally's bedroom was a more modest retreat. The voluminous canopy bed and ample wing chair by the fire demonstrate well-padded comfort. The Otises saved their best furniture and grand decorative gestures to impress their guests. Some pieces of the family's furniture remain in the home, which is otherwise furnished with eighteenth- and nineteenth-century pieces by Boston furniture makers.

While living on Bowdoin Square, Otis began his political ascent by winning a seat in the United States House of Representatives. As the area became increasingly commercial, Otis sold the home in 1801 and moved his family to a new Bulfinch-designed mansion at 85 Mount Vernon Street. Both Bulfinch and Otis were members of the Mount Vernon Proprietors, a group of early real estate developers who turned the pastureland on the south slope of Beacon Hill into Boston's most fashionable address. Ultimately, Bulfinch would design three homes for Otis, who went

on to become a United States senator and mayor of Boston. The third mansion at 45 Beacon Street overlooks Boston Common and is more than twice the size of the family's Bowdoin Square residence.

The Otises' first home led an interesting if less exalted existence after their departure. Several rooms at the rear of the second floor tell the stories of some of the other inhabitants and reflect the changes in the neighborhood. Perhaps the most colorful occupants were Dr. Richard Dixon Mott and his wife Elizabeth Mott. The couple rented a portion of the house in the 1830s, using it both for their residence and for their homeopathic practice. Richard patented the curious "Medicated Champoo Vapour Bath" to treat patients with steam infused with herbs. Although she had not earned a medical degree, Elizabeth called herself a "Female Physician" and wrote her own "medical" treatise, *The ladies' medical oracle; or Mrs. Mott's advice to young females, wives, and mothers.*

A couple of decades later, Lavina, Maria, Caroline, and Eliza Williams—four unmarried sisters—ran a genteel boardinghouse from 1854 to 1868. One small bedroom is now shown as it was comfortably furnished for a boarder. But the house and neighborhood around it continued downhill in the years after the Civil War. By the time William Sumner Appleton purchased the Otis House in 1916, the building had seen hard use and was in a deteriorated condition. The Harvard-educated scion of an old Boston family, Appleton had founded the Society for the Preservation of New England Antiquities (now Historic New England) in 1910 and purchased the Otis House for the Society's headquarters.

SPNEA's stewardship preserved the building even as its surrounding neighborhood underwent rapid change. In fact, SPNEA had barely completed several years of restoration when the house was threatened by a project to widen Cambridge Street in the 1920s. Ultimately, SPNEA moved the big brick mansion back from the street by 43 feet and placed it on a new foundation. The move took about a week—roughly seven feet per day. In the 1950s, much of the neighborhood was razed in the name of urban renewal. But the Otis House survives as a historic house museum and is still the headquarters of Historic New England, the oldest and largest regional heritage organization in the country.

Ether Dome at Massachusetts General Hospital
Bulfinch Pavilion at the end of North Anderson Street; 617-724-8009; massgeneral.org/museum; open weekdays when not otherwise in use, call to confirm; free. T: Charles/MGH

Boston kept Charles Bulfinch busy. As his buildings rose around the city, he established himself as the country's first professional architect. Bulfinch had already designed the Massachusetts State House and numerous mansions on Beacon Hill, St. Stephen's Church in the North End, University Hall at Harvard, and the

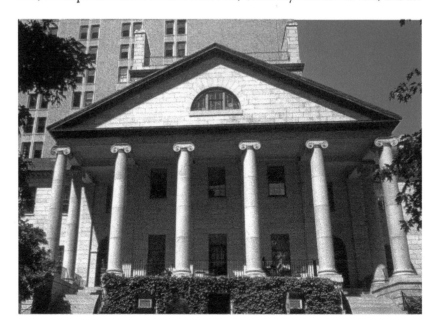

expansion of Faneuil Hall by the time his plan for Massachusetts General Hospital was accepted in 1818.

Doctors James Jackson and John Collins Warren were among the city leaders who proposed building a hospital in 1810. At the time, only New York and Pennsylvania had hospitals that provided around-the-clock care to the general public. The Massachusetts legislature moved quickly to grant a charter for the Massachusetts General Hospital in 1811. It is the third oldest general hospital in the country.

Delayed by the War of 1812, construction did not get underway until 1818. By then, Bulfinch had shifted his attention to the United States Capitol in Washington, D.C., so architect Alexander Parris stepped in to oversee the construction of Bulfinch's signature Greek Revival–style building. The hospital was constructed of great slabs of granite that were shaped at the state prison in Charlestown. That inmate labor resulted in significant savings, bringing the cost in around $70,000. The project foreshadowed things to come. With his design for Quincy Market a few years later, Parris effectively established the Boston Granite Style.

Bulfinch visited hospitals in New York, Philadelphia, and Baltimore to observe how well they functioned and used those insights to link his distinctive architectural style to practical considerations. Now called the Bulfinch Pavilion, his building is dwarfed by the modern campus of Massachusetts General Hospital. But the power of Bulfinch's design perists. The central section rises two stories above a raised basement and features a front portico with eight Ionic columns. It is capped with a square attic story with a saucer dome skylight, which served as the operating amphitheater. Wings on either side were designated as wards and sickrooms. The first patient, a man with syphilis, was admitted on September 3, 1821.

By 1846, the wings had been doubled in size, and the interior of the building had been modernized. The operating amphitheater retains its 1846 appearance as steeply raked seats rise in curved tiers on the south side of the room. The skylit dome rests on reflective copper-lined vaulting, with the operating theater directly below the oculus. The arrangement maximized light for the surgeons. It also meant that the bloodcurdling screams of patients enduring surgery without anesthesia would rise up rather than drift down to the wards below.

Things began to improve for patients and surgeons alike on October 16, 1846, when the first public demonstration of the successful use of inhaled ether as an anesthetic took place in that room. Pain relief during surgery had long been an elusive goal. Doctors had tried everything from alcohol to hashish to opium to dull the pain—all with little success. During the 1830s, ether became known as a "recreational drug," administered to willing participants during so-called "ether frolics."

On a more serious note, in 1842 Dr. Crawford W. Long of Georgia tried a minor operation on a patient who had been rendered unconscious by inhaling ether. It was successful, but Long didn't publish his results until 1848. By the middle of the decade, Dr. Horace Wells, a dentist in Hartford, Connecticut, was experimenting with nitrous oxide (sometimes called "laughing gas") to ease pain while extracting

teeth. He even presented a demonstration for Harvard Medical School. But the assembled physicians were said to cry "Humbug!' when the patient reported feeling pain, perhaps from an inadequate dose.

Wells's partner, William T. G. Morton, who had moved to Boston to establish his own dental practice and to attend the medical school, continued the quest for pain relief. Following the suggestion of chemist Charles Jackson, Morton turned to ether. His experiments on animals, his dental patients, and even himself convinced him that he had stumbled on a method to suspend sensation in patients. Morton approached Massachusetts General Hospital and asked to demonstrate his "preparation." Hospital cofounder and chief surgeon Dr. John Collins Warren invited Morton to participate in an operation scheduled for 10 a.m. on Friday, October 16, 1846.

Many of the doctors and medical students who filled the observation gallery that day were skeptical of Morton's claims. After fussing with his equipment, Morton arrived late, just as Warren was getting ready to began the operation without him. Morton grasped the hand of Edward Gilbert Abbott and assured him that he would feel no pain. Morton then placed a sponge saturated with ether into a glass globe with both a narrow and a broad glass tube attached. Abbott inhaled from the larger of the tubes and fell asleep within five minutes. Warren then removed a tumor from Abbott's neck and stitched him up. When the patient returned to consciousness, he is said to have asked if the surgery had begun and reported that he had not felt a thing. Warren announced to the spectators, "Gentlemen, this is no humbug."

The space remained the hospital operating room until 1868 and was the site of about 8,000 surgeries. Now called the Ether Dome, it was designated as a National Historic Landmark in 1965, and the Bulfinch Pavilion in 1970. Today the Ether Dome is used for classes, lectures, and meetings. But its glory day is hardly forgotten. A 2001 painting, *Ether Day 1846* by Warren and Lucia Prosperi, commemorates what Mass General has called "the greatest moment in the history of surgery." To create the 6- by 8-foot painting, the Prosperis took numerous photos as two physicians in period clothing reenacted the famous surgery.

Within two months, operations using ether as an anesthetic had taken place in Paris and London. As a plaque in the Ether Dome recounts, "Knowledge of this discovery spread from this room throughout the civilized world and a new era for surgery began."

NORTH END AND CHARLESTOWN

Paul Revere House
19 North Square; 617-523-2338; paulreverehouse.org; open year-round; admission charged. T: Haymarket

If walls could talk, the Paul Revere House would have a lot to say. The dark wooden building has been named for its most famous occupant. But even without its association with a hero of the American Revolution, the house could easily claim its place in Boston history. Built around 1680 in one of the city's earliest neighborhoods, it is the oldest house still standing in downtown Boston. Visitors can step off the sidewalk of the lively twenty-first-century North End for a rare look at early life and architectural styles in the English colony.

Boston had only been settled for a half century when the two-and-a-half story building with a pitched gabled roof and leaded casement windows rose on North Square. Modest by today's standards, it was, in fact, a spacious and fashionable home for wealthy merchant Robert Howard. The large hall on the ground floor was most likely used as both living room and dining room. Filled with fine pieces of furniture made between 1650 and 1720, the hall speaks of the taste and style of the home's first occupant.

The house was nearly a century old when Paul Revere purchased it in 1770. Following in his father's footsteps, Revere had established himself as a silversmith and purchased his first home in a neighborhood that attracted many artisans and tradesmen. Revere was 35 years old when he, his wife Sarah Orne, five of their children, and his mother moved into the house that would come to bear his name. Sarah died only three years later, and Revere soon married Rachel Walker. He and each wife had eight children, of whom eleven survived to adulthood. Between five and nine of those children lived in the house at any one time.

Some of the younger children probably slept in a small bedroom on the second floor, while older children slept in a third-floor addition that has since been removed. A Windsor rocking chair in the bedroom is thought to have been owned by Revere, and a charming sampler on the wall was stitched by a great-granddaughter.

Adjacent to the small bedroom, the much larger "best chamber" was shared by Revere and his wife. Following the custom at the time, the room was not solely for sleeping or grabbing a bit of time away from all those children. It was also a sitting room where the Reveres could entertain friends or important guests. With a canopy

bed, high chest, and scallop-edged table set for a card game, the room reflects Revere's growing wealth after the Revolution. The Windsor side chairs at the table, the wing chair, and the sewing table under the window belonged to the Revere family.

The kitchen on the ground floor may have originally been used as a back parlor or bedroom. The Reveres probably didn't convert it to a kitchen until their later years in the house. In any event, this space has a special place in American history. On April 18, 1775, Revere most likely slipped out the back door under dark of night to avoid the British soldiers gathered in North Square. He made his way to the waterfront, was rowed across the Charles River to Charlestown, mounted a horse and began his now-legendary ride to warn patriots of the British march on Lexington and Concord. Revere was stopped by a British patrol before he reached Concord, but was released after questioning and made it safely back home.

The Revere family may have lived elsewhere in the 1780s, but Revere didn't sell the house on North Square until 1800. By then he had opened a foundry that made cannons and materials for shipbuilders but is best known for its church bells. One of the largest bells hangs in the belfry at King's Chapel (see page 10). In 1801, Revere established a copper rolling mill that only a year later provided the copper sheeting for the dome of the Massachusetts State House (see page 37). When he died in 1818, Revere was a wealthy and well-respected man. He became an almost mythic figure when Henry Wadsworth Longfellow's (see page 163) poem "Paul Revere's Ride" was published in the *Atlantic Monthly* in 1861.

As other Boston neighborhoods eclipsed the North End in fashion and prestige, the fortunes of the Revere house followed those of its environs. Shortly after the Reveres moved on, their home became a boardinghouse for sailors and was later a tenement for immigrant families seeking a toehold in their new country. The ground floor was converted to shops, including, over the years, an Italian grocer, a fruit and vegetable vendor, and a candy store. A bank serving Italian immigrants and a cigar manufacturer operated out of the second floor.

The old house had been well built, but wear and tear over the years took their toll. When his ancestor's home was threatened with demolition in 1902, Revere's great-grandson John Phillips Revere purchased the property. The Paul Revere Memorial Association was soon formed to buy the building. Wasting no time, the association began restoration and reconstruction in 1907 with the aim of returning the home to its late seventeenth-century appearance. When the Paul Revere House opened to the public on April 18, 1908, it once again made history as one of the earliest historic house museums in the country.

Old North Church
193 Salem Street; 617-858-8231; oldnorth.com; open year-round; fee charged. T: Haymarket

From the beginning, Old North Church seemed to be marching toward a date with history.

When Boston's Anglican worshippers outgrew King's Chapel (see page 10), the well-established North End was selected as the site for Boston's second Anglican parish. Neighborhood residents—from artisans and merchants to sea captains and well-to-do English families—all contributed to the cost of constructing Christ Church in the City of Boston, as Old North is formally known.

The church was sited on a pasture next to the cemetery on Copp's Hill, the highest point in the North End. After the cornerstone was laid on April 15, 1723, the building began to take shape following plans by William Price, a book and print dealer. Price drew from the published designs of Christopher Wren, the definitive architect of the British Georgian style and creator of more than fifty churches in London. As a result, Old North is more attuned to Wren's graceful approach than to the more sparsely adorned four-square solidity of Boston's Puritan meetinghouses. When it was completed in 1737, the red brick church building featured a front entrance into a rectangular hall, box pews separated by long aisles, and a 100-foot-high tower. In 1740, the tower was topped with a wooden spire. Today Old North is the oldest surviving church building in Boston and the first in the English colonies to fully embrace the British Georgian ecclesiastical style.

The bells in the tower were cast in Gloucester, England, around 1745 and were the first peal of eight to reach America. About five years later, 15-year-old Paul Revere and six friends formed a guild and became the church's first bell ringers. Their signed contract called for them "once a week in Evenings to Ring the Bells for two hours Each Time." It is fair to say that the youthful bell ringer became well-acquainted with Old North's soaring height.

Revere's family were Congregationalists, so he didn't actually worship at Old North, where the parishioners were surprisingly diverse for a city with divided political allegiances. Most Anglican churches were strictly Loyalist, and Old North did boast some king-loving heavy hitters among its wealthier members, including General Thomas Gage, commander of the British forces in Boston, and Major John Pitcairn, leader of the British march on Lexington and Concord. Patriots favoring the cause of freedom also worshipped at Old North, although they were greatly outnumbered.

Members were required to purchase seating. The most well-to-do preferred the box pews, which they could decorate to their own, often quite colorful, taste. Parishioners of more modest means sat on benches in the upper gallery. Free and enslaved Black worshippers sat in the north side of the gallery closest to the pulpit.

On the night of April 18, 1775, Old North helped make history. Sexton Robert Newman and vestryman Captain John Pulling Jr. climbed to the spire of the church—the tallest spot in the city. As arranged by Paul Revere, they displayed two lanterns from a window for exactly one minute to signal that the British were moving "by sea" up the Charles River to make their way to Concord in search of weapons and supplies stockpiled by the Colonial forces. At the front of the church on the right (facing the altar) hangs a replica signal lantern presented by President Gerald Ford when he visited on the 200th anniversary of that fateful night. It marks the window where Newman and Pulling were said to have escaped into the night. In a city occupied by 4,500 British soldiers, it is almost impossible to overstate the risks that the two men took in the name of freedom. Every year, Old North celebrates their bravery with a Lantern Ceremony. In his address Ford proclaimed that "The two lanterns of Old North Church have fired a torch of freedom that has been carried to the ends of the world."

As animosity between the parishioners grew, Old North closed its doors for three years. The rector, bound by vows to the king, followed other Loyalists to exile in Canada. After the cessation of hostilities, Old North reopened as a Protestant Episcopal Church in the United States, affiliated with the Anglican community but not recognizing the king of England as head of the church. It remains an active house of worship. The building was restored in 1806, when the box pews were replaced with slip pews, and again in 1912 to 1914 when more historically accurate box pews were restored. The famous spire was blown down in 1804 and replaced several years

later with one that may have been designed by Charles Bulfinch. When a 1954 hurricane felled that spire, it was replaced with a replica of the original.

The interior was painted white during the early twentieth-century renovation. While not necessarily historically accurate, the neutral color makes a serene backdrop for some of the church's historic features, including the brass chandeliers above the center aisle. They were first lit on Christmas Day, 1724. Because the large windows are all clear glass, the interior of the church is awash with light on a sunny day and glows with nearly shadowless illumination on days with fog or overcast skies. The bust of George Washington installed in the alcove left of the altar was donated to the church in 1815. When the Marquis de Lafayette visited the church about a decade later, he is said to have declared, "Yes, that is the man I knew and more like him than any other portrait."

The church's first organ was purchased secondhand in Newport, Rhode Island, and installed in 1736. A replacement was completed by Thomas Johnson of Boston in 1759. Like any instrument in constant use, the organ has been rebuilt many times, though most of the casing and several pipes are original to the Johnson instrument. The four angels that stand on pedestals around the organ were probably carved in Belgium in the early seventeenth century. They were donated to Old North in 1746 by John Gruchy, then a member of the congregation. Tradition holds that Gruchy, the privateer captain of the brigantine *Queen of Hungary*, took them from a French ship bound for Quebec.

The Avery-Bennett clock, built by two of the church's original parishioners in 1726, is mounted on the gallery immediately beneath the organ. Though no longer keeping time, it remains a silent witness to history.

Charlestown Navy Yard

Visitor Center, Building 5, First Avenue, Charlestown (Boston); 617-242-5601; nps.gov/bost; open year-round; federal or state ID required to board USS *Constitution*; free. T: North Station

Building a new nation is a monumental undertaking. When the United States government set about creating naval shipyards shortly after achieving independence, Boston was one of the original six sites selected. It only made sense. In recognition of the city's long maritime history, Secretary of the Navy Benjamin Stoddert wrote to President John Adams in April 1800 that "Boston . . . must always remain, a Building place & a place of Rendezvous for our Navy. . . ."

Charlestown Navy Yard (originally Boston Naval Shipyard) was established that same year. It must have given Bostonians some satisfaction to site it on Moulton's Point on the Charlestown peninsula. Only twenty-five years earlier, British warships had landed here to begin the assault on Bunker Hill (see page 85).

From its original 43 acres, the Navy Yard grew to 201 acres at its peak. When it closed in 1974, the Charlestown Navy Yard had already been designated as a National Historic Landmark. Thirty acres were set aside as part of the Boston National Historical Park. Built for the ages from brick and local granite, many other Navy Yard buildings live on as offices, residences, restaurants, and a hotel. The Navy Yard is also home to two National Historic Landmark vessels, the USS *Constitution* and the USS *Cassin Young*.

The Navy Yard was always a place of hard work and innovation. Dry Dock 1, one of the first two in the country, was completed in 1833. Its first occupant was the USS *Constitution*. Over the years, its original 341-foot length grew to 415 feet to accommodate larger vessels. In the same decade that Dry Dock 1 opened, the Navy constructed the 1,360-foot-long brick-and-granite Ropewalk building. Designed by the master of the Boston Granite style, Alexander Parris, this facility manufactured all the cordage for the Navy for more than a century. Charlestown also built more than 200 ships and helped keep thousands more afloat through renovations and repairs.

It is hard to comprehend the role of Charlestown Navy Yard in American naval history. The vessels it has sent into battle have included swift sloops that hunted down pirates in the Caribbean, massive frigates that traded heavyweight blows with the British Navy in the War of 1812, capacious supply ships and refrigerated cargo vessels that backstopped troops in Europe during World War I, and swift and deadly destroyers and submarines that challenged the German and Japanese navies in World War II. Ironically, the two ships tied up at the Navy Yard piers were not built here, but they neatly bracket the historic range of United States Navy fighting ships over the years.

USS *Constitution* may be the most well-known ship in the country. Launched in 1797 from Edmund Hartt's Shipyard in the North End near the current Coast Guard station, she is one of the six original ships authorized by the US Navy in 1794. She remains the senior vessel in the fleet and the oldest commissioned warship in the world.

A mere six frigates put the American navy at a numerical disadvantage compared to the fleets of other sea powers. To compensate, one of the principal designers, Joshua Humphreys, called for vessels that would be technologically superior—effectively frigates of their day, but on steroids. They would be longer, higher, and broader, enabling them to carry more than 42,000 square feet of canvas and slice through the water at more than 13 knots. The United States Navy sought to have vessels that could outmaneuver their opponents and use superior armament to crush any opposition. Typically, the ships were fitted with thirty-two long guns effective to two-thirds of a mile and twenty heavy cannons with a range of 400 yards.

USS *Constitution* was put to the test quickly against French privateers in the West Indies and against pirates off the Barbary Coast. But she most distinguished herself during the War of 1812 when she met British frigates in three separate engagements and defeated four vessels. Her most famous encounter—and the one that earned her the nickname "Old Ironsides"—was with the British frigate HMS *Guerriere* on August 19, 1812. In thirty minutes of close-range combat, enemy cannonballs bounced off the side of *Constitution* and one of her crew was said to exclaim "Huzza! Her sides are made of iron!" *Guerriere*, on the other hand, was so damaged

that she was forced to surrender. During her career, USS *Constitution* was involved in forty sea battles without a loss. After the War of 1812, the *Constitution* served in Mediterranean, Pacific, Indian, and African waters and as a Navy training ship. She has been restored numerous times to bring her appearance back to her 1812–14 heyday.

The Charlestown Navy Yard's other resident vessel, the USS *Cassin Young*, may lack the glamour and sense of romance of "Old Ironsides," but she represents a class of warship essential to American dominance of the oceans from World War II through the Vietnam conflict. *Cassin Young* is a Fletcher-class destroyer, the main design built during World War II. In fact, Charlestown built fourteen of them. The USS *Cassin Young*, however, was constructed in 1943 by the Bethlehem Steel Corporation in San Pedro, California, and served in the Central Pacific.

The nature of naval warfare certainly changed over the centuries, but like the USS *Constitution*, the Fletcher-class destroyers were designed to be fast and fierce. They were all-purpose vessels able to fend off attacks from the surface, from the air,

or from below the waves. Designed to reach a speed of 38 knots, they carried large batteries of anti-aircraft guns, five-inch guns in enclosed mounts, ten torpedo tubes, and depth charges for flushing submarines from the deep.

The destroyers were the essential escorts for more cumbersome battleships and aircraft carriers, effectively serving as the outer perimeter of a convoy. USS *Cassin Young* saw action in seven World War II battles in the Pacific and survived two kamikaze hits. As a radar picket ship—considered the most hazardous sea duty of World War II—she provided early warning of incoming air attacks. In addition to serving as a picket ship, she escorted larger vessels, handled shore bombardments, and rescued pilots forced to ditch at sea. She patrolled Korean waters during that peninsular conflict and later deployed in the Atlantic, Caribbean, and Mediterranean before being decommissioned in 1960.

Bunker Hill Monument
Monument Square, Charlestown (Boston); 617-242-7275; nps.gov/bost; open year-round; free. T: North Station, Community College

As most Massachusetts schoolchildren know, colonial forces did not win the Battle of Bunker Hill. But the monument to the first major battle of the American Revolution was no mistake. In what was at best a hollow victory, British troops suffered severe losses at the hands of patriots who proved able to hold their own against a larger, more well-equipped enemy. To put it in modern sports terms, the underdog Americans gained the momentum.

Most Massachusetts schoolchildren also know that the battle did not take place on Bunker Hill, but on slightly lower Breed's Hill. Both the Americans and the British had their eyes on the Charlestown heights, which commanded a view of the harbor below. Fearing that the British were preparing to take control, the colonial militia acted first. On the night of June 16, 1775, a thousand soldiers from Massachusetts and Connecticut were ordered to build a fortification on the open pastures and fields of Bunker Hill.

History has never fully explained why the Americans ended up on less defensible Breed's Hill instead. But they wasted no time constructing a roughly 400-square-foot redoubt on the crest of the hill. When dawn broke on a newly fortified Boston, the British moved quickly to crush the colonial upstarts. They bombarded Breed's Hill with cannon fire from their men-of-war in the harbor and from their position on Copp's Hill across the Charles River in the North End. The colonial troops still managed to add to their cover by building a breastwork down the northeastern slope of the hill.

In the early afternoon, 2,400 British troops began a two-pronged assault on the American position. Rattling their bayonets in chilling rhythm, they advanced from the southeast and from the north along the banks of the Mystic River. The fortifications held and the British were forced to withdraw. They gathered reinforcements for one more assault and finally breached the walls. With ammunition running low, the Colonial soldiers were forced to flee.

In the course of the two-hour battle, the British suffered 1,000 killed or wounded. Of the estimated force of 1,400–1,800 Americans, 300 to 500 were killed, wounded or captured. In exactly nine months, the British would sail out of Boston for good.

The blood was spilled on Breed's Hill, but somehow the name Bunker Hill stuck and so the battle—and the monument which commemorates it—are known to this day.

The first monument on the site was a modest 18-foot tall wooden pillar topped with a golden urn. The Freemasons erected it in 1794 to honor their comrade Joseph Warren, a physician and commissioned officer. Warren, who ignored the privilege of rank to fight and die beside his men, was one of the early heroes of the Revolution.

Feeling the need for something more truly monumental, the Bunker Hill Monument Association was founded in 1823. On the fiftieth anniversary of the battle, another Revolutionary War hero, the Marquis de Lafayette, laid the cornerstone for a granite obelisk. The Frenchman, who had risen to the rank of Major General in the Continental Army, was on what would become his final tour of the country he fought to establish.

Despite such an auspicious start, construction of the monument languished as the cash-strapped Monument Association was forced to sell much of its battlefield property to raise funds. The Bunker Hill Monument was finally dedicated on June 17, 1843. It marks the center of the hastily constructed redoubt. Granite markers barely visible on the grassy expanse identify each corner of the fortification, as well as the spot where Warren fell.

The Bunker Hill Monument was built for the ages. Constructed of enormous granite blocks from the Quincy quarries south of the city, it rises 221 feet and is 30 feet square at its base. Solomon Willard, who designed the monument and supervised the construction, even helped devise a railway to transport the huge granite blocks from the quarry. The Bunker Hill Monument reigned as America's tallest monument until it was dethroned by the Washington National Monument more than four decades later.

The 4-acre Charlestown site is surrounded by an iron fence with four gates named for the American military units from Massachusetts, Rhode Island, and Connecticut that fought in the battle and for Colonel Richard Gridley's engineers who supervised construction of the fortifications. From the Massachusetts gate, steps lead to the bronze statue of Colonel William Prescott, principal commander of the American forces. One of the enduring bits of Revolutionary lore is attributed to Prescott. Knowing the wild inaccuracy of the muskets and his soldiers' inability to reload as the Redcoats rushed their position, he is said to have instructed his troops, "Don't fire until you see the whites of their eyes."

A statue of Joseph Warren and other artifacts sit in the single-story granite lodge that was constructed adjacent to the monument in 1901. The lodge grants access to an iron staircase that spirals up to the observation platform at the top of the monument. The 294-step climb is rewarded with a sweeping harbor view and a fuller understanding of why the little hill figured so prominently in America's fight for independence.

BACK BAY AND THE FENWAY

Boston Public Garden

Bordered by Boylston, Charles, Arlington, and Beacon streets; friendsofthepublicgarden.org; open year-round; free. Swan Boats operate mid-April to early September; 617-522-1966; swanboats .com; admission charged. T: Arlington

The Boston Public Garden and Boston Common are separated by a three-lane stretch of Charles Street—and by nearly two centuries. When cows began to graze on the terra firma of Boston Common (see page 1) in the 1630s, the land on its western edge was a marsh fed by the waters of the Charles River at high tide. Residents, including a young Benjamin Franklin (born in Boston in 1706), made good use of this miasma for hunting, fishing, and digging clams—and when they found time for fun, for swimming or ice-skating.

As the city grew, the marshlands became more nuisance than resource. In the 1820s, a mill dam extending along Beacon Street to neighboring Brookline reduced the marsh to foul, pungent mudflats. The city began to fill in the area and even contemplated selling the new land as house lots. Nothing really happened until the late 1830s, when the city leased 20 acres to a private association called the Proprietors of the Botanic Garden in Boston. The group built a greenhouse and added ornamental trees and plants until financial trouble forced them to return the land to the city in 1852. But their efforts were not in vain. The proprietors succeeded in establishing the second public park in Boston—and the first public botanical garden in America. Moreover, they awakened Bostonians' appetite for an island of beauty in the heart of the city.

The people of Boston were not alone in their yearning for green spaces. New York City began development of Central Park at about the same time and Boston's leaders were clearly feeling the pressure to keep up. An 1859 City of Boston Report summed up their concerns and hinted at the competition: "While other cities are expending fabulous amounts in the improvements of parks, squares, gardens, and promenades, what should we do? To be behind in these matters would not only be discreditable to our city, but positively injurious to our commercial prosperity, and in direct opposition to the wishes of a vast majority of our citizens."

The city answered that rhetorical question later that same year. An act of the Legislature set aside the area between Charles and Arlington streets for public use in perpetuity. A public competition for the new park's design selected architect George

F. Meacham, awarding him a $100 prize and the opportunity to leave his mark on the city. As filling of the 24-acre parcel was completed over the next decade, Meacham's landscape design slowly took shape.

The two most striking features of Meacham's plan are as delightful today as they were during Victorian times. The sinuous lagoon at the center is surrounded by graceful trees and spanned by an arching cast-iron pedestrian bridge. The meandering designs of Meacham's paths almost compel a leisurely pace. They literally encourage folks to stop and smell the roses.

Meacham's fanciful design reflected a city with the time, money, and inclination to indulge whimsy and aesthetic delight. Long gone was the survival-mode mentality that created Boston Common as grazing land. Instead, Boston was eager to present itself as genteel and cultured. Not coincidentally, the Public Garden would become the graceful gateway to the Back Bay. As landfill progressed westward from the Public Garden, a neighborhood of stately Victorian homes rose on the new land and eventually eclipsed the wealth and social status of Beacon Hill.

To fill the formal flower beds of Meacham's design, gardeners turned to the burgeoning horticultural know-how of the city, hybridizing plants and creating novel techniques for mass propagation. At the same time, horticultural researchers were collecting and bringing home exotic plants from around the world. While many were planted in the Arnold Arboretum (see page 185), many others became fixtures in the Public Garden. By 1880, about 1,500 trees, including many imported exotic specimens, made the Public Garden an oasis of shade and color. Today, the Boston Parks and Recreation Department grows about eighty species of plants for the flower beds and works with the Friends of the Public Garden to care for the mature specimen trees and to conduct regular planting and maintenance.

The first monument to appear in the Public Garden was the 1868 Ether Fountain, which memorializes the first successful use of ether as a surgical anesthetic at nearby Massachusetts General Hospital in 1846 (see page 65). The figures at the top represent the Good Samaritan caring for an injured stranger he had met on the road. That metaphorical monument was followed quickly by Thomas Ball's towering equestrian bronze statue of George Washington that was unveiled in 1869. It greets visitors as they enter the Public Garden from Arlington Street. Surrounded by blooming tulips in the spring, the statue is one of Boston's favorite photo ops.

Many other monuments and fountains have followed over the years, but none rivals the popularity of the Duckling Sculpture at the corner of Beacon and Charles streets created by Nancy Schön and installed in 1987. Inspired by the 1941 book *Make Way for Ducklings* by Robert McCloskey, Schön depicts the mother mallard and her brood of eight ducklings as they make their way toward their eventual home in the lagoon. Little hands have burnished the bronze of the ducklings' beaks, and admirers of all ages often dress the ducklings in Boston sports gear or warm hats and scarves in cold winter weather.

These days, however, ducks are not the most famous waterfowl at the lagoon. That honor belongs to a pair of white mute swans who spend their winters at the Franklin Park Zoo, but who nest on the lagoon's banks during the warmer months. In early May, Bostonians mark the return of the swans to the lagoon with a parade through the Public Garden led by a brass band. Awaiting their arrival is the fleet of six Swan Boats.

Robert Paget introduced this giddy bit of Victoriana to the lagoon in 1877. After several years of offering rowboat rides, he decided to create something novel—a catamaran-style boat powered by a foot-propelled paddle wheel. He covered the mechanism with a big white swan inspired by Richard Wagner's opera *Lohengrin*. In that story, the titular knight comes to the rescue of Princess Elsa by sailing across a river in a boat drawn by a swan. The oldest boat remaining in the fleet was built in 1910. Each of the six vessels can carry up to twenty-five passengers on a fifteen-minute cruise around the lagoon and back nearly a century and a half to fanciful Victorian days.

Gibson House Museum
137 Beacon Street; 617-267-6338; thegibsonhouse.org; open year-round; admission charged. T: Arlington, Copley

Catherine Hammond Gibson was a widow in her fifties, living comfortably on Beacon Hill, when she became a Boston pioneer.

In 1859 she purchased a lot in the first block of the newly filled land in the Back Bay and commissioned architect Edward Clarke Cabot to design a home for her and her son Charles Hammond Gibson. The new home was one of the first to rise in the Back Bay. Moreover, Catherine was one of the few women to own property in what is now celebrated as one of Boston's most architecturally distinctive neighborhoods.

Catherine had married sugar trader John Gardiner Gibson in 1833, and the couple spent the first two years of their marriage in Cuba. When her husband died in 1838, she was left to raise their two sons, though only Charles, born in 1836, was living when Catherine made her bold move.

The cramped city of Boston had high hopes for the new land that was rising from the fetid mudflats of tidal Back Bay. Architect Arthur Gilman, an admirer of French city planning, laid out arrow-straight avenues crossed at regular intervals with residential streets and specified plenty of open green space. The neighborhood was designed for Bostonians like the Gibsons. Although they were not in the highest echelons of Boston wealth, the upper-middle-class family boasted a fine pedigree of

patriots of the Revolutionary War and successful merchants and traders. Architect Edward Clarke Cabot channeled Gilman's sense of order in the design of Catherine's red brick and brownstone home. Cabot, who had designed the Boston Athenaeum (see page 59) a decade earlier, referenced the French Empire style in the home's symmetrical and modestly ornamented facade.

The six-story building, a twin to the adjoining home owned by a nephew, was a bit grand for two inhabitants. The layout reflected the Victorian preference for neatly

separating public and private domains as well as providing space for the servants who were considered essential for maintaining a gracious home. The ground and top floors were strictly for those servants. The kitchen, laundry, and sleeping area for male servants occupied the lowest level. From the kitchen, women would climb a flight of ninety-four steps to the four bedrooms on the top level. The first and second floors, where family members would both relax and entertain guests, were the most elaborate, while the third and fourth floors were reserved for bedrooms. The home boasted all the modern conveniences including central hot-air heating, gas lighting, and plumbing

Catherine also hoped to fill the home with more family members. She had a bit of a wait until Charles, a cotton broker, married Rosamond Warren in 1871. Rosamond burnished the family's pedigree with her lineage to China traders and physicians, including Dr. Joseph Warren, a hero of the Battle of Bunker Hill (see page 85). Charles and Rosamond's two daughters and son grew up in the family home. In the 1880s, the six family members were attended by seven live-in servants.

The restrained exterior of the Gibson House belies its Victorian heart. The interior has all the hallmarks of Victorian taste: fine finishes, lavish furnishings, and a profusion of artwork and decorative objects that by today's standards seems an embarrassment of riches. Few surfaces were left unadorned. In fact, the house represents almost a century of changing fashion, particularly the tastes of its two matriarchs. Shortly after Catherine's death in 1888, Rosamond undertook a series of renovations to update the interior.

The unusually large front entrance hall with grand staircase perhaps best represents the merging of styles of Catherine and her daughter-in-law Rosamond. The dark walnut woodwork and heavy furniture are original features of the home, while Rosamond added the embossed and gilt wallpaper that would catch and reflect light. The entry hall led into the formal dining room, which was used both for family meals and to entertain guests. Although Rosamond did remodel the room with new carpet and gold burlap pattern wallpaper, it remains the room that most bears Catherine's stamp.

On the second floor, the comfortably overstuffed library with walls covered with family portraits was deemed the men's parlor. The music room, where the family often entertained, was the largest room in the house. Rosamond transformed it by having the woodwork and some of the furniture painted white and by adding yellow- and rose-colored vertically striped wallpaper. Catherine moved from the master bedroom on the third floor to a smaller room on the fourth floor so that her daughter-in-law would have the larger room as her private sanctuary. It is probably a good thing, since the master suite may be the only bedroom large enough to accommodate the remarkable fifteen-piece faux bamboo-style bedroom set that Rosamond

received as a wedding gift from her mother. As was common at the time, her husband Charles maintained a separate, but connecting, bedroom at the front of the house.

Rosamond continued to live in the house after her husband's death in 1916. Shortly before her own demise in 1934, the couple's son Charles Hammond Gibson Jr. returned to the family home. Known to all as "Charlie," the younger Gibson had eschewed a career in business to lead a more colorful life as a writer, horticulturist, preservationist, and advocate for public parks. A gay man who styled himself a bon vivant, Charlie also had a fond attachment to the more decorous Victorian lifestyle of his home's early years. To delve deeper into Charlie's life and the gay subculture of his time, the museum offers the specialty tour called "Charlie Gibson's Queer Boston." Charlie's 1899 travelogue *Two Gentlemen of Touraine* is believed to be a fictionalized account of his most significant romantic relationship. He also published a second travelogue, *Among French Inns*, as well as several volumes of poetry. Charlie turned his father's bedroom into a study, where he could entertain close friends or settle at his desk to write.

During a 1936 visit to Delaware, he learned of cousin Henry Francis du Pont's intentions to turn his family home into a museum (now Winterthur Museum, Garden & Library). That same year, Charlie founded the Gibson Society so that his family home could be likewise preserved. The Back Bay row house may not exactly rival 175-room Winterthur, but its artifacts and social history make it a time capsule of the tastes and lifestyles of three generations of well-to-do Bostonians.

Charlie wrote some of the early tour scripts. Some apocryphal accounts describe him roping off the furniture and asking guests to sit on the stairs while they drank martinis made with his own bathtub gin. Even taken with a grain of salt, the tale captures the spirit of a man who cherished his image as a dandy as much as he loved his home's decorous niche in Boston history. By the time Charlie died in 1954, just four days before his eightieth birthday, he had witnessed sweeping changes to his neighborhood. As families left the city behind for life in the suburbs, the Victorian row houses were being divided into apartments or sold to universities and other institutions. But three years after his death, the Gibson House Museum opened to the public. One of the few intact single-family residences in the neighborhood—filled with the family's prized possessions—it captures a vanished way of life.

Church of the Covenant
67 Newbury Street; 617-266-7480; cotcbos.org; open for tours May through October; by donation. T: Arlington, Copley

Boston sparked quite a building boom in the late 1850s when it began filling in the pungent mudflats of the Back Bay to create what would become the city's most fashionable neighborhood. Marching from the Public Garden (see page 89) and across Massachusetts Avenue to Charlesgate in the Fens, the stately town houses are practically a chronological catalog of Victorian architectural styles and tastes. But

homeowners weren't the only ones to embrace the Back Bay. Many church congregations also jumped at the opportunity to leave cramped quarters in the old city to create statement buildings on Boston's new architectural stage.

First organized in 1835, the Central Congregational Church laid the cornerstone for a new home on the corner of Newbury and Berkeley streets in 1865. The congregation engaged Richard M. Upjohn, one of the leading ecclesiastical architects of the day, to design a building in the Gothic Revival style that was then in fashion for churches. Constructed of local Roxbury puddingstone, Upjohn's daring design was erected in a mere three years despite being the width and height and half the length of a Gothic cathedral. Touching all the bases of the architect's signature style, it boasted pointed arches, flying buttresses, and a main entrance on Berkeley Street with a three-part porch and fleur-de-lis Gothic trefoil arches. Monumental in scale and exquisitely articulated in detail, the church reflected the congregation's aspiration to greatness. It was an unmistakable landmark visible from the Public Garden. Indeed, its 236-foot spire remained the highest built structure in the city until the advent of the skyscraper era in 1915.

Upjohn's interior featured two side aisles and is most notable for the graceful piers that run the length of the nave. Unseen, the same structure is echoed beneath the church, with piers extending through the filled land to solid earth below. Tour guides often say that the construction is so sound that the ceiling would stand even if the walls were removed. Pews and woodwork were of black walnut and the walls

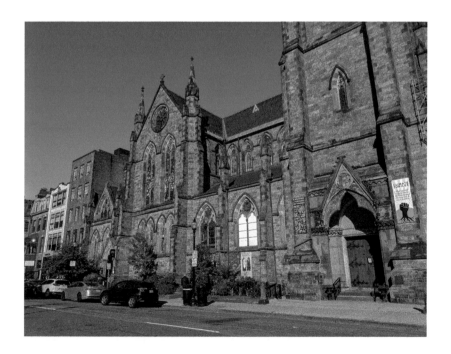

were painted a neutral color. Stained glass windows followed the medieval style of decorative abstract designs stenciled on the glass. The church was lit by gaslight.

For all its original glory, the church interior had begun to lose its luster and cachet by the late nineteenth century. Later additions to the neighborhood, including

Trinity Church (see page 108) and Old South Church, both in Copley Square and both also National Historic Landmarks, had set new standards for distinctive architecture and interior decoration. To maintain and build its congregation—and to satisfy future brides who dreamed of walking down a center aisle—Central Congregational went all in on a floor-to-ceiling renovation by the Tiffany Glass and Decorating Company, the most famous and accomplished firm in the country. From 1894 to 1896, the sanctuary was completely stripped and rebuilt in one of the Tiffany company's most sweeping commissions.

Several of Tiffany's leading designers worked with local craftsmen to achieve an overall vision of artful harmony and spirituality. Radiating like the spiritual heart of the building, the massive (6 foot by 12 foot) electrified lantern hanging in front of the chancel is the focal point of the church. It was designed for the 1893 World's Columbian Exposition in Chicago, where the Tiffany company made a big splash with an elaborate display that even included a chapel. The lantern was designed by Jacob A. Holzer, who also directed the sanctuary project. The light is often called the grandfather of all Tiffany art glass lamps. In addition to its colorful art glass, it features bronze filigree and sculpted female figures representing the Seven Angels of the Seven Churches from the Book of Revelation. Antiquity and modernity meet in an unintentionally witty coincidence: The interlinked and outstretched hands of the angels hold heavenly fire—or more accurately, light bulbs.

Close examination of the sanctuary reveals that no detail was too small for the attention of the Tiffany artists. The space was reconfigured with a center aisle, two side aisles, and a vestibule at the main entrance. All the black walnut interior was replaced with quarter-sawn oak, including wainscoting, a new pulpit, and pews with embossed copper medallions at the ends. The ceilings were painted blue with gold stenciled borders and the wall behind the altar was stenciled in a brocade-like pattern. Tesserae mosaic panels behind the communion table, along the length of the altar railing, and on the stair risers reflect every glimmer of light in the space, creating an almost mesmerizing glow. Overhead, the filigreed hammer beam trusses at ceiling height provide elaborate heavenly decoration.

Although the work was mostly completed by 1896, the forty-two stained glass windows were fabricated and installed between 1893 and 1914 as funds allowed. The windows epitomize the innovation and artistry of Louis Comfort Tiffany and his firm and are the sanctuary's crowning glory. (Four windows to the right of the altar and a partially obscured rose window from the earlier Gothic interior are lovely in their own right, though their technical virtuosity cannot approach the later Tiffany glass.)

The clerestory level features twenty-two ornamental windows. At 13 feet high, they create a visual march of color and pattern along the long walls of the sanctuary. The twenty more elaborate figure windows range from 11 to 22 feet high. They achieve their design clarity through the use of nine or more types of specialized glass and their depth of color through the overlay of up to five layers of glass. The firm was especially known for its deft use of ribbed "drapery glass" to capture the folds of fabric and to convey the contours of the body beneath the clothing.

Several windows are unique to the church, including the trio of Joshua Before Ai, Jonathan and David, and Abraham Leaving Ur—which represent Hope, Love, and Faith respectively. Designed by Holzer, who was Tiffany's mosaic master, they

demonstrate a brilliant use of small pieces of glass assembled for dramatic effect. They are also famed for the Tiffany sunset glass of the evening sky.

To the left of the chancel, Frederick Wilson's four-window grouping of women of the Bible shows Dorcas (raised from the dead as recompense for her generosity to the poor), Mary of Bethany (sister of Lazarus), Deborah (judge and warrior dressed in armor), and Miriam (sister of Moses, shown dancing ecstatically). They represent Charity, Devotion, Courage, and Joy with a sinuous pre-Raphaelite grace.

Perhaps the most complex windows are Wilson's interpretations of Revelation in the Glorified Church and the Ascended Christ. The largest windows in the church, the pair features more than eighty saints and angels arrayed around two central figures. The Glorified Church is embodied as a feminine figure with a golden crown of twelve stars and a gown decorated with pomegranates, symbol of the Resurrection.

Two of the congregation's favorite windows are on the right as you enter from Berkeley Street. The Sparrow is Wilson's sweet evocation of the young Jesus as a carpenter, contemplating the sparrow that only he can see. The drapery glass of his clothing and the mottled confetti glass of the background are unostentatious examples of tour-de-force glass art. Just kitty-corner, the Hospitality Window (or Emmaus) was designed by Richard Sperry. He chose broad, bright colors to depict the tale of Emmaus welcoming a stranger to his home—a stranger who turns out to be Christ on the day of the Resurrection. The window is emblematic of the welcome the congregation extends to all.

In 1932, Central Congregational federated with Boston First Presbyterian Church under the new name of Church of the Covenant. Its members have remained dutiful stewards of their historic building and sanctuary as an artistic expression of spirituality. In 2012, Church of the Covenant was designated as a National Historic Landmark in recognition of its unique status as the "largest intact Tiffany-designed ecclesiastical interior in its original location in America."

Trinity Church

260 Clarendon Street; 617-536-0944; trinitychurchboston.org; open year-round for guided and self-guided tours; admission charged. T: Copley

On a sunny day, the reflection of Trinity Church sparkles in the mirrored glass of the 790-foot tower that soars above it on Copley Square. When celebrated modern architect Henry N. Cobb set about designing what is still the tallest building in Boston for the John Hancock insurance company, he made sure that his deceptively simple skyscraper did not steal the spotlight. Cobb deferred to an earlier master, H. H. Richardson, and to one of Boston's most iconic landmarks, Trinity Church.

"I was very interested in . . . the problem of how cities can grow and accept tall buildings in a way that is not damaging to older buildings, but actually works in concert with them," Cobb reflected several decades after the Hancock Tower (now called 200 Clarendon Street) was completed in 1976. "In the case of Trinity Church and the Hancock Tower, the tower is designed in such a way that the church is reaffirmed as the center of a composition, whereas the tower is very much a peripheral element."

Cobb's masterful piece of city planning was hardly the first recognition of Trinity's special qualities. In 1885, the church was selected as one of the ten best buildings

in America by the American Institute of Architects (AIA). At the time, Richardson's dignified yet joyous model of ecclesiastical architecture had anchored one side of Copley Square for less than a decade. Trinity was designated a National Historic Landmark in 1970. By 1985, the church was the only member of the original AIA list still in the top ten.

Seemingly impervious to architectural trends, Trinity Church is arguably Richardson's greatest work and one of the most influential buildings in the United States.

It epitomizes the architect's signature style—a confident union of clay tile roofing, roughly finished stone blocks in multiple colors, and weighty arches reminiscent of French Romanesque churches. From Boston, "Richardson Romanesque" spread across the country as monumental libraries, churches, schools, and even railroad stations.

Trinity Church, now an Episcopal congregation, was initially gathered in 1733 as Boston's third Anglican parish. Seeking to move from downtown Boston, the members purchased a block in the Back Bay in 1872 and awarded the architectural commission to Richardson. Like most of the Back Bay, the church lot was little more than recently filled swamp. To prevent his building from sinking into the ooze below, Richardson directed workmen to drive thousands of wooden piles through the subterranean mud to support a network of granite pyramids. On those rocks, the church would rise.

Richardson worked closely with his friend Phillips Brooks, the rector of Trinity from 1869 to 1891. Realizing that the church would stand in splendid isolation on its side of Copley Square, the architect proposed a Greek cross design. Rather than the more traditional English Gothic model of a long nave and three aisles, Trinity would have four nearly equal legs projecting from the soaring central portion that would sit beneath a grand bell tower modeled on the Old Cathedral in Salamanca, Spain. The high but broad arches would give the building a Byzantine volume, as if it encapsulated a bit of soaring heaven.

That voluminous construction with its inspirational dome left massive wall areas and broad supports between and under the windows. Richardson engaged artist John La Farge to inject rich color into the interior of the church. La Farge had never worked on such a large project, but readily accepted the challenge to generate, as he put it, "the feeling that you are walking into a painting." Working with a small group of artists, La Farge managed to cover 21,500 square feet with murals and decorative details in only five months—just in time for the consecration of the church in February 1877.

Trinity's stained glass collection ranks among the best in the country. But on the day of the consecration, only the Baptism window in the chancel had been installed. The other spaces were filled with clear glass until donors stepped forward and more pieces could be commissioned. Many of the most established American and European studios are represented on Trinity's walls, including William Morris & Co, which executed four designs by Pre-Raphaelite painter Edward Burne-Jones. La Farge created five windows using his revolutionary technique of layering opalescent glass to achieve subtle shading, complex colors, and an illusion of depth. Phillips Brooks had charged the artist to give him something inspirational to look at when he preached. La Farge more than delivered with his masterpiece, Christ in Majesty.

A towering Christ stands tall in blue and burgundy robes in the central panel, which is flanked by aquamarine lancet windows.

By all accounts, Brooks hardly needed extra encouragement. One of the most charismatic and physically imposing preachers in nineteenth-century Boston, Brooks was a gifted orator. He could transport his parishioners on the wings of his words, which spewed out at a rate of 213 per minute, according to one awed listener. Alas, there is no audio, but a 1910 statue of Brooks by Augustus Saint-Gaudens, installed on the Boylston Street side of the church, captures the preacher in action.

The bell-like construction of the vaults gives Trinity stupendous acoustics. A preacher's voice, the joined chords of the choir, and the deep pipes of the organ all resonate in praise. The church's annual concert series always includes several evenings of Christmas carols as well as a performance of Handel's Messiah. From September to June, Friday noontime organ concerts feature musicians from the United States and around the world.

Boston Public Library
Copley Square; 617-536-5400; bpl.org; open year-round, check website for schedule of art and architecture tours; free. T: Copley

The Great and General Court of Massachusetts was ahead of its time when it established the Boston Public Library in 1848, thus creating the first large free municipal library in the United States. Fifty years later, the city ratified and expanded on that grand gesture by building what its architect dubbed a "palace for the people" with the words FREE FOR ALL inscribed above the doors.

Visitors who enter from Dartmouth Street are forgiven if they think they are in a Renaissance palazzo rather than a library. The building itself is such a meticulously crafted work of art that it would take a lifetime to absorb all its fine details. As the late poet and Nobel laureate Seamus Heaney once noted, those who enter the BPL "are actually beating the bounds of human creativity."

The library had fairly modest beginnings. It opened in 1854 with 16,000 volumes housed in a former school building on Mason Street. Less than five years later, it relocated to a larger space on Boylston Street across from the Boston Common before finally finding its permanent home on Copley Square.

Architect Charles Follen McKim was challenged to create a building that would equal, but not overshadow, H. H. Richardson's Trinity Church (see page 108) on the opposite side of Copley Square. McKim drew inspiration from Renaissance palazzos, a mid-nineteenth-century Parisian library, and even from Richardson's design for the Marshall Field Wholesale Store in Chicago. Construction of the Boston Public Library began in 1888. McKim called on the skilled Italian construction workers and artisans who were building Boston's grand private homes to help bring his vision to life. Completed in 1895, the stately white marble building anchored its side of Copley Square with an air of quiet confidence. The horizontal facade is pierced with a row of thirteen arched windows and three arched doorways. When McKim's building was designated as a National Historic Landmark in 1986, the National Park Service called it "the first outstanding example of Renaissance Beaux-Arts Classicism in America."

Taking a page from Renaissance-era patrons, McKim also recruited the leading artists of the day to contribute to the building's rich decoration and symbolism. Daniel Chester French's sculpted bronze doors representing Music and Poetry, Knowledge and Wisdom, and Truth and Romance make a fitting ceremonial entry

to the marble-laden interior. McKim hand-selected the yellow marble for the walls of the grand staircase in the entry lobby. Two sculptures of seated lions, the work of Louis Saint-Gaudens, watch over patrons as they ascend and descend the staircase that author Henry James described as "a high and luxurious beauty." The lions were a memorial gift from the survivors of two Civil War units and were installed before the sculptor was able to polish the marble. The donors favored the raw look, and so the lions remain. Rubbing the lions' tails, by the way, is considered good luck.

France's leading muralist, Pierre Puvis de Chavannes, created the murals that wind up the staircase and along the second-floor corridor. Of his only mural work outside France, the painter noted that "I have sought to represent under a symbolic form and in a single view the intellectual treasures collected in this beautiful building." The main panel, *The Muses of Inspiration Welcoming the Spirit of Light*, captures the nine muses of Greek mythology in flowing white gowns greeting a nude youth amid an idyllic setting of olive and laurel groves on Mount Parnassus.

Painter and illustrator Edwin Austin Abbey, who excelled at depicting literary and historical scenes in the Pre-Raphaelite style, created the sumptuous series of murals of the Arthurian legend of the *Quest for the Holy Grail* in the second-floor room now named for him. The images are so accomplished and powerfully narrative that a viewer would never guess that they represented Abbey's first mural commission.

Many late nineteenth-century artists viewed mural painting as the highest form of the painter's art. John Singer Sargent spent nearly three decades working on his mural sequence, the *Triumph of Religion*, located on the third floor in a tall, narrow space of his own design. Known primarily for his society portraits, Sargent hoped to enhance his reputation and secure his legacy with this major project. Alas, the artist died before he was able to paint his vision of the Sermon on the Mount for the east wall. The space remains blank to this day.

Palaces may be for nobility, but the sheer majesty of the Boston Public Library can make any commoner feel like a king. That's especially true in Bates Hall, the main reading room. It stretches the length of the Copley Square facade and features a beautifully detailed 50-foot-high barrel vault ceiling, sandstone walls, terrazzo and marble floors, and 10-foot-tall English oak bookcases designed by McKim. Readers sit at long wooden tables illuminated by Arts & Crafts brass lamps with green glass shades.

The great surprise at the heart of the building is the central courtyard. The arcaded promenade, modeled on a Roman palace, protects readers from both sun and rain, and the fountain in the middle offers the cooling sound of water on even the hottest of days. The courtyard was immediately embraced as a tranquil escape from the bustle of the city. Bostonians, in fact, were so effusive in their praise that the *Boston Daily Globe* was prompted to write that "the courtyard . . . is fully worthy of all the hysterical appreciation that has been bestowed on it."

The courtyard statue of *Bacchante and Infant Faun* by Frederick MacMonnies was not as enthusiastically received. McKim donated the artwork to the library in memory of his wife. Proper Bostonians declared that the image of a nude dancing woman holding a bunch of grapes in one hand celebrated drinking and exposed her child to debauchery. They succeeded in getting it removed in 1897. McKim donated the statue to the more open-minded Metropolitan Museum of Art, which calls it "one of the most vibrant images in American art." More than a century passed before

calmer heads prevailed and a copy cast from the original claimed its rightful place in the courtyard.

Stopping in the courtyard eases the transition between the McKim building and the 1972 modern addition by architect Philip Johnson. More recent renovations to the McKim building carved out space for a casual cafe and the elegant Courtyard Tea Room. Taking afternoon tea at a table overlooking the courtyard is one of the most gracious ways to spend an afternoon in Boston.

Symphony Hall

301 Massachusetts Avenue; 617-266-1200; bso.org; Boston
Symphony Orchestra concert season September through April;
Boston Pops concert season December and May through June;
admission charged; check website for schedule of free tours.
T: Symphony

Symphony Hall may predate the phrase, but it is nonetheless one of the best examples of "purpose-built architecture." It marks the first time that the scientific study of acoustics dictated the design of a concert hall. That radical approach paid off.

Symphony Hall is routinely lauded as one of the most acoustically resonant concert halls in the world. Inaugurated in 1900, Symphony Hall is where the Boston Symphony Orchestra grew into a world-renowned ensemble.

Henry Lee Higginson founded the Boston Symphony Orchestra in 1881. The avid music lover, former Civil War major, and successful businessman hoped to elevate Boston's already strong music scene with a permanent orchestra like those in the great music capitals of Europe. For its first two decades, the BSO performed in downtown Boston at the Boston Music Hall. When that building was threatened with demolition, Higginson purchased a lot at the corner of Massachusetts and Huntington avenues. Symphony Hall was one of the first buildings to rise on the recently filled land that the city envisioned as the site of a new cultural district.

To create a permanent home for his orchestra, Higginson assembled his dream team. The Norcross Brothers construction firm, which had built Trinity Church (see page 108), handled the engineering. The steel-frame building—one of the earliest in the city—rests on piles sunk into the fill. Architect Charles Follen McKim, who had designed the Boston Public Library (see page 116), created a restrained Italian Renaissance Revival–style building. The red brick structure with limestone trim sits on a base of gray Quincy granite. Finally, Higginson engaged Wallace Clement Sabine, then an assistant professor of physics at Harvard with an interest in acoustics, to make sure that the concert hall would present his orchestra in full-throated clarity and resonance.

Sabine conducted acoustical tests in other Boston buildings and studied the design of some of Europe's most celebrated concert halls. He concluded that a simple rectangular shape, wider than it is tall, would be the acoustical sweet spot—the side walls and ceiling reflecting sound back to the middle of the space where the audience was seated. Moreover, he suggested that the side walls and ceiling angle slightly outward from the stage and that the stage itself be somewhat raked. The resulting shape—a subtle cone—would function like a loudspeaker and project the sound into the seats of the auditorium.

Patrons originally climbed the granite steps on the Huntington Avenue side of Symphony Hall to enter through seven pairs of oak double doors. When some of the stairway was lost to a street modernization project, the main entrance was moved to Massachusetts Avenue, originally the carriage entrance. The central archway features elaborate limestone trim topped by a lyre carved from the stone.

Higginson, who routinely covered the shortfalls between the orchestra's revenues and expenses, had warned McKim from the outset that the budget for the project would be tight. In the end, McKim had to abandon his plans to incorporate other decorative elements, including niches for sculpture, into the facade. Even in the concert hall itself, the ceiling ornaments and statue-filled wall niches serve science more than art by breaking up sound waves to avoid the harsh bounce from a flat surface. The ornate grilles on the balcony fronts serve the same purpose, while the balconies themselves are intentionally shallow, lest they swallow the sound and create dead spots.

The original Hutchings organ was replaced by the Aeolian-Skinner Organ, Opus 1134, in 1949. Certain elements of the first organ—the facade, pipe-work, and some mechanical components—were incorporated into the new instrument. But the instrument was tailored to Symphony Hall's acoustics, resulting in an acoustical marriage still celebrated by organ builders and acoustical engineers.

The auditorium was built with one other ingenious feature. Four years after founding the BSO, Higginson introduced the Promenade Concerts (now the Boston Pops) of light classics and popular music to provide a longer playing season for musicians and to attract a broader audience. Pops patrons favor cafe-style seating, so the concert seats were devised so they could be removed to the basement for storage via a hydraulic lift.

Symphony Hall's inaugural concert on October 15, 1900, featured a performance of Beethoven's *Missa Solemnis* in D major, a piece little known to American audiences. It seems only fitting, since Beethoven occupies a place of honor in the hall. His name is carved on a tablet in the elaborate proscenium arch festooned with gilt ornamentation.

That first concert set the BSO on its path as a trailblazer in the world of orchestral music. Not only did it reinterpret classical music for a Boston audience, it also introduced Bostonians to a broad range of works by French and Russian composers as well as the Germans who had dominated the orchestra's original repertoire. By the early twentieth century, the BSO had also begun to champion American composers and modern music. Under Serge Koussevitzky's leadership, the BSO launched an extensive program of commissioning new work, building the career of Aaron Copland and discovering Leonard Bernstein. The BSO gave world premieres to five works by signal modernist Igor Stravinsky and American premieres to six more.

Unlike many symphony orchestras, the BSO and the Pops record in their performance hall. Audio engineers work in a state-of-the-art studio in the basement of Symphony Hall and might use up to fifty microphones to capture the subtleties and nuances of a BSO concert for radio broadcast and for public release. Symphony Hall's defining feature—its one-of-a-kind sound—has reached music lovers around the world.

Jordan Hall at New England Conservatory

30 Gainsborough Street; 617-585-1260; necmusic.edu; free and ticketed concerts. T: Symphony

Musicians toting instrument cases scurry across the intersection of Gainsborough Street and Huntington Avenue, proclaimed the "Avenue of the Arts" by the City of Boston. Each year a new wave of aspiring professionals brings fresh talent, dreams,

and ambitions to the New England Conservatory, America's oldest independent school of music.

New England Conservatory was founded in 1867 by Eben Tourjée and Robert Goldbeck. Composer and pianist Goldbeck left a year later to found another conservatory in Chicago while Tourjée, an organist as well as a music educator and choral conductor, stayed on to stabilize the fledgling Boston school. He served as director and president until 1890. Classes were originally held in the Music Hall

in downtown Boston, now the Orpheum Theater, before the school relocated to the South End in 1882. About two decades later, the conservatory built its permanent home in the Fenway, the last neighborhood in Boston to be created by filling tidal swamps and mudflats of the newly dammed Charles River. The formal and restrained Classical Revival buildings speak the visual language of formality and metrics, the aesthetic qualities that music and mathematics share. But their form can be deceptive—a distinct creative buzz fills those halls.

NEC trains and nurtures musicians in classical, jazz, contemporary improvisation, world, and early music. In 1969, then-president Gunther Schuller introduced jazz to the curriculum, making NEC the first major classical conservatory to offer a concentration in this distinctly American music. Schuller himself was an agnostic about musical forms, having played French horn for the Cincinnati Symphony and the Metropolitan Opera for a quarter century while also joining Miles Davis in 1949 and 1950 for the seminal jazz recording *Birth of the Cool*.

Today's NEC student body numbers about 720 undergraduate, graduate, and doctoral students from around the globe. The 225 faculty are equally cosmopolitan, hailing from several countries and performing as guest artists in the world's concert halls. Of course, they also have strong connections in Boston. Roughly half the musicians who make up the Boston Symphony Orchestra either studied at NEC or have taught there.

One of the prized resources for NEC students and faculty is Jordan Hall, the school's premier concert hall. Built at a cost of $120,000 and opened in 1903, the hall's design predated the widespread application of architectural acoustic science—a field that only debuted three years earlier at Symphony Hall (see page 121). Yet the creators of Jordan Hall got almost everything right, creating what is widely regarded as one of the acoustically finest performance spaces in the world. In 2019, NEC also installed a world-class modern audio system to augment the hall's natural sound. In 1994, both New England Conservatory and Jordan Hall were recognized as National Historic Landmarks.

The conservatory presents more than 600 free concerts per year, many of them at Jordan Hall. The performances range from solo recitals to full-blown orchestral concerts. Chamber music, jazz, and opera also get their turns in the spotlight. For the student body, the chance to perform for a live audience is on a par with the education gained from hearing other performers, including the many visiting guest artists.

The space looks as lovely as it sounds with its decorative figures, gilt, and Neoclassical majesty. When the lights dim and the musicians take the stage, the hall seems to clear its metaphorical throat and begin to sing. With its organ pipe backdrop and resonant floor, the stage projects the music into the chamber of the hall where the rounded walls and coffered ceiling focus the sound into a vast column. Instead of emanating from the stage, music seems to descend from above and wash over the hall, leaving the audience rightly entranced.

MARITIME BOSTON

Long Wharf and the Custom House Block
Boston Harbor at the foot of State Street; open year-round; free.
T: Aquarium

In the Age of Sail, Long Wharf was Boston's highway to the world. The longest of the town's more than eighty wharves, it reached—if only metaphorically—all the way to London and the Far East. Sea trade literally put the American colonies on the map, and for the first half of the eighteenth century, Boston was North America's preeminent port. Even after New York and Philadelphia burgeoned in the latter part of the century, Boston remained a key trading port until well after the Civil War.

It is no exaggeration to say that Long Wharf was the keel of the shipping trade that made Boston's early fortunes. The era of massive East Indiamen carrying square miles of sail into the wind or Donald McKay's swift Boston clippers sailing around the globe is long past, but Long Wharf remains Boston's jumping-off point to the

sea. Water taxis skitter off to Charlestown and Logan Airport. Ferries shuttle day-trippers to the Boston Harbor Islands. Powerful catamarans whisk whale watchers to the offshore feeding grounds of the Stellwagen Bank Marine Sanctuary.

Captain Edward Noyes began construction of Long Wharf in 1710 and finished the initial project in 1721. Further extensions continued until 1756, when the wharf finally reached a half mile into the harbor. Its simply descriptive name barely hints at the audacity of such a project in colonial Boston. Details of Long Wharf's construction do not survive, but limited archaeological digs suggest that it was erected on a combination of wooden and granite pilings. It reached far enough into the harbor that water depths were roughly eighteen feet, accommodating the deepest-draft vessels of its day. They docked at the end of the wharf, sharing space with the town battery that defended Boston against invasion by sea.

Smaller vessels docked at berths along one side of the wharf, while warehouses and stores lined the other side. Ships could dock at Long Wharf and unload their cargo directly to warehouses, bypassing the need for tenders to ferry cargo from vessels anchored offshore. Traders then marched up State Street to pay their taxes and clear their goods at the Custom House, thereafter continuing up the street to see their bankers. Boston's ships landed madras from India, silks from China, spices from the Far East, and all manner of exotic goods that gave the city a cosmopolitan air. But history also records that Boston's shipping merchants engaged in the

Triangle Trade that enslaved people from Africa—a legacy that the city still struggles to properly acknowledge.

Even apart from its mercantile activity, Long Wharf was a witness to history. After capturing the French bastion of Louisbourg in Canada, the victorious British fleet landed at Long Wharf in 1758 to cheering Boston crowds. Ten years later, the British landed an occupying force at Long Wharf in the buildup to the American Revolution. As they came, so they went, when George Washington forced the evacuation of British forces from Boston on St. Patrick's Day in 1776. That summer, a ship from Philadelphia arrived at Long Wharf with the news of the Declaration of Independence. Through the Revolution, Long Wharf was home to privateers and blockade runners. During the War of 1812, it berthed the USS *Constitution* (see page 79), the frigate built in a North End shipyard in 1797.

When Boston shifted to other industries after the Civil War, Long Wharf concentrated on more modest coastal trade and fishing. In the first decades of the twentieth century, the fishing fleet moved to the new Fish Pier in South Boston and the wharf—once the grandest built structure in Boston—was dwarfed by Boston's first skyscraper, the sixteen-story Custom House Tower.

Today Long Wharf is less than half its original length, yet the few historic buildings at the end of the modern wharf recall its finest years. A restaurant since the 1970s, the Chart House exemplifies the modest scale of the brick warehouses constructed at the end of the eighteenth and beginning of the nineteenth centuries.

Essentially three conjoined buildings extensively renovated as a single structure, the two easternmost sections appear to date from Colonial times. The one closest to land is often considered an early 1830s design by prominent Massachusetts-born architect Isaiah Rogers.

Past the Chart House, the massive Custom House Block, completed in 1848, speaks the same heroic Greek vocabulary as Quincy Market (see page 23). It is the survivor of several mid-century Greek Revival granite buildings that came to characterize Long Wharf's warehouses. Exemplifying the Boston Granite school of architecture, it displays both the ground-floor monolithic columns and the unadorned geometry that made this style a nineteenth-century precursor to utilitarian Modernism.

To appreciate how Long Wharf shaped modern Boston, an observer need only walk to the end of the existing pier, turn back from the harbor view, and gaze instead on the modern city. It rises up from the water, its stepping-stones of buildings like the ascending ring of seats in a grand amphitheater. Boston was born of the sea when the world came ashore at Long Wharf.

Boston Light
Little Brewster Island, 617-223-8666; nps.gov/boha or bostonharborislands.org; visible on Lighthouse Cruises, inquire about guided visits. T: Aquarium

In fair skies or foul weather, Boston Light welcomes mariners seeking safe harbor. That kind of maritime signpost is precisely what Boston's merchants were seeking when they petitioned for a light station in Boston Harbor in 1713. With the town's early fortunes inextricably tied to maritime trade, the government of the Province of Massachusetts Bay agreed to erect a lighthouse on Little Brewster Island.

Mariners were already familiar with Little Brewster, the outermost above-water point of a rocky ridge that separates Boston Harbor from Quincy Bay. When they sighted the island—about eight miles east of Boston's wharves—they knew they were close to home. But they still had to thread the needle of the mile-wide channel south of Little Brewster and north of Point Allerton on the mainland in Hull. Hidden rocks and shoals made the passage challenging in any weather and treacherous during a windstorm or fog. Ships that had sailed halfway around the world foundered even as their sailors had spotted distant land and were dreaming of a warm welcome ashore.

Builders selected the highest point of Little Brewster Island—about 18 feet above sea level—for America's first lighthouse. Constructed of roughly mortared irregular rubble stone, the circular tower gradually tapered as it rose to its full height of 60 feet. On September 14, 1716, Boston Light became operational as candlelight

from its tower beamed into the dark to mark the entrance to Boston Harbor. Three years later, the lighthouse keeper established another first by using a cannon to warn ships off the rocks during periods of heavy fog.

In splendid isolation on the outer reaches of offshore land, Boston Light was the far-off sentinel that guarded the throat of the harbor. It was as important as any fortress, maybe more so. Rather than guard against enemies, it welcomed homeward-bound vessels and friendly trade from distant ports.

After a peaceful half century or so (apart from some quickly repaired damages from oil fires), Boston Light became a strategic prize during the Revolutionary War. British forces seized the island in 1774, making them the gatekeepers of the harbor. Colonial raiding parties twice tried to put Boston Light out of commission by setting

it afire. The British ultimately caused the greatest damage. They blew up the lighthouse on a time-delayed charge when they evacuated Boston in March 1776.

When Boston Light was reconstructed in 1783, it rose to 75 feet high and was illuminated by four fish-oil lamps. The Commonwealth of Massachusetts used the original plans and what remained of the lower portion of the tower for the new building. But Boston Light could no longer claim to be the oldest lighthouse in the country. The 1764 Sandy Hook Light in New Jersey now has that distinction.

At the end of the eighteenth century, the new United States government took control of all navigational aids, including Boston Light and eleven other lighthouses. Over time, Boston Light was reinforced with horizontal steel bands (now aluminum) to contain structural decay of the rubble stone walls. A clockwork revolving

mechanism for the lens was installed to create a flashing light. The poor lighthouse keeper had to wind it every four hours. The flashing pattern enabled mariners to differentiate Boston Light from beacons on the mainland north and south of the harbor, allowing them to triangulate their positions. Climbing to the light was made easier when an interior spiral staircase was installed in the nineteenth century. The ascent of seventy-six stairs followed by two ladders remains daunting.

The greatest change to Boston Light came in 1859, when additional construction raised the tower to its present height of 89 feet. The extra headroom was required to accommodate the massive second-order crystal-and-brass Fresnel lens that stands 11 feet high and weighs two tons. The combination of 336 prisms and a dozen circular lenses reflects and refracts light to focus a narrow, concentrated beam into the oceanic dark. The massive lens remains in operation, slowly spinning so that every ten seconds the 1.8 million candlepower light flashes for seven-tenths of a second, a signal visible for 27 nautical miles.

Only 800 feet long and 250 feet at its widest at low tide, Little Brewster shrinks to an acre and a half at high tide. Yet the tiny island enjoyed quite a construction boom at the end of the nineteenth century as the wooden keeper's house, a boathouse, a brick cistern, an oil house, and a building to hold the fog signal were all erected on this outermost rock. They all remain today. The keeper's house was finally outfitted with indoor plumbing in 1960.

The United States Coast Guard took control of Boston Light in 1939. The light was extinguished during World War II but has operated without pause since July 1945. It was electrified in 1948 and fully automated in 1998, almost a decade after all other American lighthouses. Now the light remains on both day and night.

Nonetheless, a lighthouse keeper remains on duty. In November 1989, the late Senator Edward M. Kennedy sponsored a bill requiring the light to be, in the tone-deaf parlance of the time, "permanently manned." There is a certain symmetry to Kennedy's legislative action: The site of America's first staffed lighthouse is also the last site in America with a lighthouse keeper. History was made again in 2003 when the first woman keeper, Sally Snowman, arrived on Boston Light to follow in the footsteps of the sixty-nine men and their families who had called Little Brewster home for nearly three centuries.

Schooner *Roseway*
Courthouse Docks, Boston Harbor; 617-755-7241; worldoceanschool.org; public sails June through early September; admission charged. T: Courthouse

Schooner *Roseway* was built to last. She was launched in 1925 from the Essex shipyard of John F. James & Son and is a prime example of the proud wooden boatbuilding tradition of the Massachusetts North Shore. Lawyer Harold F. Hathaway

commissioned the vessel and is said to have harvested the white oak for her planking from his own property in Taunton. He is also said to have named *Roseway* for a "female acquaintance" known for getting her own way.

The two-masted ship is 137 feet long and carries 5,600 square feet of sail. She is classified as a fishing-style schooner yacht, a rather clumsy description that does neatly summarize her dual purpose. *Roseway* did land a record catch of 74 swordfish in a single day in 1934, but she was really built for speed. Hathaway had caught the "racing fever" that spread through Gloucester after fishermen in Halifax, Nova Scotia, challenged their New England counterparts to a series of fishermen's races in 1920. The spirited contests were held off Halifax and off Gloucester through 1938. It is not clear how often—or how well—*Roseway* performed in competition, but she certainly was a showpiece with varnished rails and stanchions. She spent winters in a specially constructed house and avoided the rough-and-tumble of schooners that spent more time fishing than racing.

In 1941, Hathaway sold his ship to the Boston Pilots, and *Roseway* began a new career as a pilot boat. She served the pilots who helped vessels thread the channel in and out of the port of Boston. *Roseway* was often anchored off The Graves island to greet ships approaching Boston Harbor. Her sturdy construction and diligent maintenance helped her withstand rough weather. The pilots who served aboard her

valued *Roseway's* speed and ease of handling almost as much as they appreciated her live-aboard comforts.

Roseway's job became much harder in May 1942 when she was commissioned as a Coast Guard Reserve Craft. With a gray paint job, CGR 812 painted on her bow, and a 50-caliber machine gun on her deck, she guided ships and convoys through the anti-submarine nets and minefields that protected Boston Harbor from enemy ships. *Roseway* rejoined the Boston Pilots in November 1945 and served until 1972 when she was replaced by a steel power boat. She was the last sailing pilot schooner in service in the United States, and her retirement marked the end of an era.

In 1973, *Roseway* began yet another new career as a member of the schooner fleet in midcoast Maine, cruising the coast to give landlubbers a taste of the seafaring life. The handsome vessel was a hit at maritime festivals and gatherings of tall ships. She even had a star turn in a television version of Rudyard Kipling's *Captains Courageous*, which was filmed in Camden, Maine, in 1977.

Roseway was donated to World Ocean School in 2002. Students from the United States and abroad board her to learn new skills, forge new friendships, and build their confidence. After roughly a century afloat, *Roseway* no longer has to endure harsh New England winters. She splits her time between Saint Croix, United States Virgin Islands, and Boston, where she is usually moored near the John J. Moakley United States Courthouse from June through early September. After morning educational programs, *Roseway* takes passengers on public sails in the afternoon. Sailing Boston Harbor at sunset is a special treat.

Nantucket Lightship/LV-112
Boston Harbor Shipyard & Marina, 256 Marginal Street, East Boston; 617-797-0135; nantucketlightshiplv-112.org; open for tours April through October; admission charged. T: Maverick

At its peak in the early 1900s, the United States Lightship Establishment boasted fifty-one "floating lighthouses" stationed at some of the most dangerous waters along the eastern seaboard and the Pacific coast. Often moored where it was impossible to build a lighthouse, these lightships guided vessels through narrow approaches to channels and harbor entrances and steered them clear of shifting sandbars and hazardous reefs.

Of all the assignments that a lightshipman might draw, the Nantucket Shoals Station was the most remote and most treacherous. An 1843 report served notice to the United States Congress that "the shoals of Nantucket are known and dreaded by every navigator on the Atlantic seaboard." When the Lightship Station was finally established in 1854, its beacon of flashing white light—visible for 14 miles—must have been a welcome sight to those nervous mariners. Moored as far as 47 miles out

to sea, the Lightship Station guided tankers, freighters, and even luxurious ocean liners through one of the world's busiest transatlantic shipping lanes. Its beacon was the first thing vessels entering the United States would see as they headed toward the port of Boston or the Ambrose Shipping Channel into New York harbor. Departing ships would turn their backs on the light as they headed out into the Atlantic.

Over the years, eleven lightships served on the Nantucket Shoals. It was the final lightship station in operation in the United States when it was replaced by a 42-foot-high navigational buoy in 1983. All eleven endured fierce storms with howling winds and turbulent seas. Even on relatively calm days, the area was often shrouded in fog.

The fog was especially thick on May 15, 1934, when the RMS *Olympic*, sister ship of the RMS *Titanic*, rammed Lightship No. 117 midships. Dwarfed by the massive ocean liner, the lightship sank within minutes; only four of her eleven crew members survived. The worst lightship disaster in the United States only added to the infamy of the Nantucket Shoals.

The Lightship Establishment was determined to build an indestructible ship to replace No. 117 on the Nantucket Shoals. Of the $500,000 in reparations paid by

the White Star Line, $300,000 was used to commission what was the most expensive lightship at the time. Launched from the Pusey and Jones Shipbuilders in Wilmington, Delaware, in 1936, Lightship No. 112 was also the largest such vessel ever built in the United States. At 148 feet long, LV-112 was built to survive whatever Mother Nature might throw her way—and to withstand a collision without sinking. She had a riveted and welded steel hull, double-plated bow and stern, steel fenders above and below the waterline, six exits to the upper deck, and an air whistle to warn ships approaching too near. Like all lightships, she had two steel pole masts mounted with lights—one in operation and one as a backup.

By the time she was decommissioned in 1975, LV-112 had set the record for the longest service on the Nantucket Shoals Light Station. She also served as a guard ship off Portland, Maine, during World War II. During thirty-nine years on the lonely and weather-buffeted Nantucket Shoals, LV-112 proved her durability. She only once sustained major damage. Her bridge and pilothouse were stove in during Hurricane Edna, the second of two powerful hurricanes to strike the East Coast within ten days of each other in 1954.

Of the 179 lightships that once beamed through the dark, it is estimated that fewer than twenty remain. As the replacement for the lightship destroyed by an ocean liner, LV-112 may be the most famous of that already rather select group. After she went out of service, LV-112 spent time in several different ports before returning to her home port of Boston, where she had been assigned to the United States Coast Guard First District headquarters. Now a floating museum, the exterior of the lightship has been largely restored and work on the interior continues as funds allow.

Christ Church

Zero Garden Street, Cambridge; 617-876-0200; cccambridge.org;
open for worship and by chance. T: Harvard

The city of Cambridge takes great pride in Christ Church. The active Episcopal parish occupies the oldest church building in the city. Historians consider the structure a resonant reminder of early life in colonial Massachusetts. Architects, on the other hand, point to the elegance inherent in its simple design. The congregation and the building, however, were hardly so well-received in the early years.

A group of wealthy merchants had fairly modest ambitions when they commissioned Peter Harrison to design a church building in 1759. Members of the Church of England, they had grown tired of traveling by carriage and ferry to Sunday services at King's Chapel (see page 10) in downtown Boston. They wanted their own, more convenient, house of worship.

Peter Harrison, one of the most accomplished of the largely self-taught architects of colonial New England, had designed the granite King's Chapel in the Georgian style only a decade earlier. But his Cambridge clients were more interested in keeping down costs than in making an architectural statement. By 1761, Harrison's more modest wooden structure, about 45 feet wide and 60 feet long, had risen across from Cambridge Common, the heart of civic life.

Classical elegance wed to an almost Puritan plainness produced a relatively unadorned, harmonious house of light. A square three-story belfry tower tops the structure. Large arched windows march in a neat line along each side. The light from those clear glass panes highlights the restrained grace of the interior. A processional line of columns on each side of the center aisle creates a stately rhythm while seeming to support the roof on each side of the church's barrel-arch ceiling.

The early religious life of Christ Church was cut short in 1774. As the Revolutionary War loomed, the pastor and many of the parishioners—all Tory supporters of King George III—either decamped back to England or fled to Canada. A year later, the Continental Army requisitioned the building as a barracks. At the request of Martha Washington, a service was held in Christ Church on New Year's Eve 1775. Observers at the time noted that Mrs. Washington wore a peach satin gown and that General George Washington was accompanied by a military escort with fife and drums.

Three years later, Christ Church opened again for the funeral of a British pris-oner. Anti-British sentiment was so high that townspeople used the opportunity to enter the church and cause considerable damage. A bullet hole in a vestibule wall is said to date from the mayhem. Christ Church remained in a sorry state until services were resumed in 1790, following the 1789 separation of the American Episcopal Church from the Church of England. Yet the congregation quickly rebounded and grew rapidly in the decades leading up to the Civil War.

Over the years, the congregation altered the interior of the building to make more room and to satisfy changing tastes. In 1820, the simply adorned Doric-style capitals on the columns were replaced with more elaborate scroll-like capitals in the Ionic style. At the same time, the columns, which had risen from the floor, were elevated onto pedestals. Like many colonial-era houses of worship, Christ Church originally featured high box pews that were purchased by members of the congre-gation. In 1853, the wood from those pews was used to create the slip pews where worshippers still gather today.

In one of the more ambitious projects, the building was lengthened by 23 feet in 1857. Unless visitors look closely at the columns, they would probably never know that the chancel and one pair of columns were moved forward to make room for two additional sets of columns and two windows. The new columns were made from ship's masts and have a smoother finish than the hand-hewn originals. No traces of one of the most unfortunate remodeling efforts remain. In the 1880s, the interior was painted red and green and adorned with angels great and small to satisfy flamboyant Victorian taste. Today, the interior color scheme of white and cream with dove-gray trim reflects the coherent simplicity of the architecture and the transparency of the faith.

One other significant change is more audible than visible. To celebrate the church's centennial, a group of Harvard students donated the thirteen-bell Harvard Chime. The single bell that called people to worship for the first century was recast to become part of a harmonious set that rings out the hymn "Gloria in Excelsis Deo." Their sound is not merely limited to worship services. Every year on Harvard Commencement Day, the bells at Christ Church and throughout the city and campus joyfully peal to send the young scholars out into the world.

Harvard University Campus Walking Tour
Start at Harvard Square; 617-495-1573; harvard.edu/visitors; open daily; free. T: Harvard

The "Colledge at Newtowne" had but one building to its name when it was founded in 1636 to educate colonial New England's clergy. By the time an architecture program was introduced in the late nineteenth century, Harvard University had amassed an impressive group of buildings arrayed around its leafy green inner sanctum. Four buildings have been designated as National Historic Landmarks, and seeking them

Massachusetts Hall

Memorial Hall

out is a good way to penetrate the inner heart of the oldest university in the United States.

More than twenty wrought iron and brick gates connect Harvard Yard to the outside world. Enter through the one across several lanes of traffic from the First Parish Cambridge and you will find yourself in the Old Yard, a former grazing ground and the oldest part of the university. Directly to your right, Massachusetts Hall, completed in 1720, was the college's fifth major building and is the oldest to survive. Harvard president John Leverett designed the four-story red brick structure in the early Georgian style. Its handsome clock, first installed in 1725, looks out on what was originally the center of the town of Cambridge. (The current clock dates from 1992.)

Massachusetts Hall has proven to be remarkably adaptable. The building took a bit of a beating during the American Revolution, when more than 600 members of General George Washington's regiment used it as a barracks. Records show that the Commonwealth of Massachusetts had to reimburse the school for the damages caused by the troops. Massachusetts Hall has also been put to more gentle uses as a dormitory, lecture hall, and observatory. Legend holds that Harvard undergraduate John Adams signed his name in the basement, but no one has yet located the signature of the second United States president. Today Massachusetts Hall houses a small group of freshmen along with the office of the university president and other top administrators.

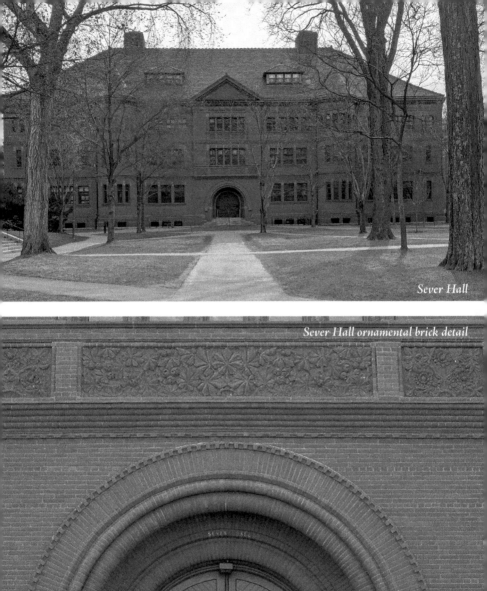

Sever Hall

Sever Hall ornamental brick detail

Follow the pathway across the Old Yard to reach University Hall, easily recognizable as one of the few granite buildings in a sea of red brick. In 1812, Harvard called on alumnus Charles Bulfinch, the already distinguished architect of the Massachusetts State House (see page 37), to design a new building that would reflect the school's lofty academic aspirations. Bulfinch offered three options and was paid $100 for his efforts. University Hall was substantially finished by 1814, when Bulfinch assumed supervision of final details. Designing for a new century, Bulfinch turned his back on the campus tradition of red brick to create a solemn and dignified building constructed for the ages in ashlar-cut white granite quarried in Chelmsford.

University Hall originally served as classrooms, dining rooms, and chapel. President John Thornton Kirkland was particularly keen on gathering all members of the university for prayer, but undergraduates seemed to relish the four dining rooms. Each class had its separate facility, with circular openings in the walls to allow some communication from room to room. Bulfinch probably never imagined that the openings would prompt students to engage in what the *Harvard Gazette* once called "legendary interclass food fights." It just goes to show that even students at one of the most prestigious universities in the world can't be serious all the time.

The interior of University Hall has been modified over the years to accommodate a gymnasium, kitchens, laboratories, laundries, and lecture halls. Today it houses meeting rooms and administrative offices, including the office of the dean of the Faculty of Arts and Sciences. It is often a focal point for student activists whose

University Hall

Statue of John Harvard

causes chronicle changing times. A 1969 sit-in protested the Vietnam War. Another in 2015 demanded that Harvard divest its fossil fuel holdings.

University Hall is also the backdrop to Harvard's most famous photo op. Nearly every campus visitor pauses in front of the bronze statue of John Harvard to grin sheepishly while rubbing his toe. The statue was created by sculptor Daniel Chester French in 1884 and installed in front of University Hall in 1924. When Harvard, a young clergyman, died in Charlestown in 1638, he bequeathed half his estate and his library of 400 books to the fledgling school. In one of history's most famous "naming opportunities," the school honored Harvard's generosity with a name change.

Walk around to the rear of University Hall (where privies and pigsties once sat) and you will enter what was long called "the New Yard," where Harvard Commencement ceremonies are traditionally held. Sever Hall is straight ahead, with 1931 Memorial Church to the left and Widener Library to the right. Opened in 1915, Widener memorializes Harry Elkins Widener, a member of the class of 1907 who died aboard the RMS *Titanic* in 1912. It is the centerpiece of Harvard's library system, the third largest in the country.

Harvard turned to another prominent architect for Sever Hall, the first major building on the eastern side of Harvard Yard. Just a year after H. H. Richardson's Trinity Church (see page 108) opened for worship in 1877, construction began on his design for Harvard's new classroom building. The architect had literally made a name for himself with his signature "Richardson Romanesque" style of granite and brownstone buildings. At Harvard, he nodded to tradition by choosing red brick for the three-and-a-half story structure. But he elevated the normally mundane material to new heights. Admirers have counted as many as sixty different shapes of brick in the building facade. Robert Campbell, the former architecture critic of the *Boston Globe*, once noted: "It is only when you look closely that Sever begins to sing. It is a symphony of all the things that you can do with brick."

The complex patterns of the brick are further accented by bricks carved with floral designs. Cylindrical towers add dimension to the front and rear facades and allow the building to echo the late medieval mien that the architect so admired. To give students hurrying to class a sense of ceremony and purpose, Richardson created a deeply recessed archway at the front entrance. One does not merely go in the door, one enters the body of the building at its navel.

Continue behind Sever Hall to exit Harvard Yard onto Quincy Street. The Harvard Art Museums are directly across the street. To the right, the 1963 Carpenter Center for the Visual Arts is the only building in North America designed by French architect Le Corbusier.

Turn left instead and then left again at the corner onto Broadway. From the broad sidewalk, you will get one of the best overviews of massive Memorial Hall. Selfie taken, you can cross the concrete Science Center Plaza for a closer look at one of the most distinctive buildings anywhere on the Harvard campus.

The dust had barely settled from the Civil War when fifty alumni banded together to raise funds to honor Harvard casualties of the conflict. They chose two Harvard graduates, William R. Ware and Henry Van Brunt, as architects. The pair envisioned Memorial Hall as a cathedral in High Victorian Gothic style. Construction began in 1870 and was completed in 1878.

The red and black brick building with a five-story central tower dominates the triangular space between Cambridge, Kirkland, and Quincy streets. In just eight years of construction, it created the kind of complex visual mass that most monasteries or cathedral complexes take eight centuries to accrete. Its unusual jumble of multicolored rooflines made it an instant landmark for Harvard and its Cambridge neighbors. Drawing on the conventions of a cathedral, Ware and Van Brunt designated the nave as a dining hall and the apse as a theater. The transept holds the main entrance and the actual memorial hall.

Visitors can often enter the memorial transept on weekday afternoons. Once your eyes have adjusted to the low light, you will be able to pick out the details of the marble floor, vaulted wooden ceiling, and enormous stained glass windows. The transept's raison d'être, however, are the twenty-eight white marble tablets set into black walnut paneling along the walls. They record the names of the 136 Harvard men, including Robert Gould Shaw (see page 4), who sacrificed their lives for the

Union cause. (More than three hundred Harvard men also fought for the Confederacy. Sixty-four of them perished in the conflict.)

Entry to Sanders Theater is through the transept. The 1,000-seat theater hosts university lectures and performances that are often open to the public as well as performances by local arts organizations. The seven-sided space is accented by stained glass windows and topped by a vaulted ceiling with wooden ribs. It is such an uplifting environment that audience members can overlook the rather cramped seats. It doesn't hurt that Sanders also has excellent acoustics. The late folksinger (and Harvard dropout) Pete Seeger described performing in Sanders as "like singing in a bathtub." He meant it as a compliment.

The lower level of Memorial Hall seems to have led a life of its own. Originally, it was relegated to kitchens, bathrooms, and storage. But in 1940, part of the area was outfitted as the Psycho Acoustic Laboratory to conduct hush-hush research on ambient noise and crew communication in combat vehicles and aircraft. From 1946 to 1964, the psychology department occupied some of the space. It was here that psychologist B.F. Skinner conducted early experiments with conditioned behavior.

Today, the lower level holds classrooms, music practice rooms, and the Cambridge Queen's Head Pub, where members of the Harvard community can kick back and relax. So far, no food fights have been reported.

Harvard Stadium
Harvard Athletic Complex, 65 North Harvard Street, Allston (Boston); game tickets: 617-495-2211 or tickets.gocrimson.com/online.

Harvard and football go way back. Members of the freshman and sophomore classes began to meet in an annual contest more than a century before the university built Harvard Stadium in 1903. The young men played with such violent abandon that a New York magazine once termed their competition "a Spanish bull-fight." Around campus it was known simply as "Bloody Monday."

By 1858, things were so out of control that *Harvard Magazine* declared that players were "in that state of irresponsibility and uncontrol which has been the parent of so much evil in the world," and concluded that "few things are more deplorable than to see God's image mauled and beaten." Two years later the faculty voted to ban the sport.

But the nascent game of football was not to be denied. Students who had played what became known as the "Boston game" in their preparatory schools brought the sport back into the groves of academe in the early 1870s. They followed rules similar to rugby. Players were allowed to pick up the ball to run or to pass it laterally or

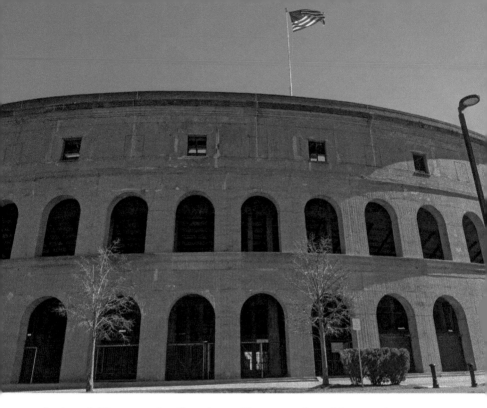

backward. They were also allowed to tackle any member of the opposing team, not just the ball carrier.

Players were so wed to their particularly physical game that Harvard declined to join Yale and several other colleges in intercollegiate competition using rules more closely derived from soccer. Instead, Harvard welcomed McGill University for two games in 1874. Harvard won both games, one played by its rules, and one played by rugby rules. But the Harvard team's dark pants, white undershirts, and magenta (not crimson) headscarves were no match for the spiffy English uniforms of McGill. By the time the two teams met the next year in Montreal, the Harvard men had proper uniforms—and were again the victors.

One of collegiate football's most storied rivalries finally began on November 13, 1875, when the Harvard Crimson and the Yale Bulldogs faced off in New Haven, Connecticut. The teams played by Harvard's rules, and the visiting team prevailed. Yale bested Harvard on the field the following year. Yale may have won the battle, but Harvard won the war. That year Yale and the Intercollegiate Football Association agreed to play by the rugby-like rules.

Harvard teams were a dominant force in the late nineteenth century, but their rundown wooden football stands were an embarrassment. Despite some concerns about the undue influence of sports in academia, the members of the Class of 1879—in true school spirit—stepped in to donate a new stadium as their twenty-fifth anniversary gift to the school. It would occupy the same site on the opposite banks of the Charles River, a short walk over a bridge from the main Cambridge campus.

For a university known for its architectural specimens, the goals for the stadium were surprisingly modest: a relatively inexpensive yet attractive structure that could hold up to Boston's tough winter weather. The finished structure, however, far

exceeded initial aspirations. Lewis F. Johnson of the civil engineering department made the radical proposal to construct the stadium of giant concrete slabs reinforced with steel. Architect Charles F. McKim, who had designed the Boston Public Library (see page 116), wed the new technology with inspiration from antiquity to create a massive, yet elegant Classical-style amphitheater, complete with two tiers of arches on the exterior. Interior seats consisted of concrete shelves that flowed in steady increments from the heights down to the playing field. The stadium rose in less than five months.

The horseshoe-shaped building is 573 feet long and 420 feet wide. When it was completed in 1903, Harvard Stadium was the world's largest building made of reinforced concrete. The first college stadium in the United States, it became a model for others around the country.

It may also have shaped the evolution of the sport of football. Several years after the stadium opened, a commission considering rules reforms chose to legalize the forward pass rather than make the playing field wider to encourage more lateral passing. Many sports historians believe the decision was made because the field at widely admired Harvard Stadium could not be enlarged.

Over the years, Harvard Stadium has hosted political rallies, rock concerts, Class Day gatherings, and even performances of the play *Agamemnon* by Aeschylus, complete with horses, chariots, and a Greek temple. Rugby and soccer games and even ice hockey have been played on the field, which also served as home for Harvard track and field until 1984. Both men's and women's lacrosse teams also play at the stadium. The Boston Patriots, forerunners of the New England Patriots, called Harvard Stadium home for their 1970 season.

But Harvard Stadium's true calling is as home field of the Harvard Crimson football team. On opening day November 14, 1903, Harvard lost to Dartmouth. But overall, the Crimson have dominated at home, playing 719 games through the 2019 season and compiling a record of 454 wins, 231 losses, and 34 tie games.

The Harvard Crimson and the Yale Bulldogs always meet for the much-anticipated last game of the season. "The Game" alternates years between Cambridge and New Haven. Harvard has enjoyed some winning streaks and even famously scored 16 points in the last 42 seconds when the teams faced off in 1968. The outcome so stunned the dominant Yale team that the *Harvard Crimson* declared victory: "Harvard Beats Yale 29–29."

Yale, however, holds the winning record. Through the 2019 season, the Bulldogs have notched 68 victories to the Crimson's 60. The teams have also tied eight times. But as every sports fan knows, there is always next year.

Harvard Stadium will be ready.

Longfellow House Washington's Headquarters National Historic Site

105 Brattle Street, Cambridge; 617-876-4491; nps.gov/long; open for guided tours late May through October; free. T: Harvard Square

Over two centuries, only four families called the mansion at 105 Brattle Street in Cambridge home. But what stories they left behind!

John Vassall had the home built in 1759 in the Georgian style favored by the English well-to-do. Having amassed his fortune in the Jamaican sugar trade, Vassall

was a staunch supporter of the British king. He settled with like-minded folks along "Tory Row," a stretch of Brattle Street that begins behind Christ Church (see page 149) and extends about a mile out of Harvard Square. The Vassall house was set back from the street on a long, green lawn and perched on a raised terrace that afforded a distant view of the then-tidal Charles River. Vassall, his wife Elizabeth, and their seven Cambridge-born children lived here until they fled to England in 1774 one step ahead of the Revolution.

Ironically, George Washington was the next occupant of Vassall's home. The general arrived in Cambridge in July 1775 to assume command of the newly formed Continental Army. He quickly selected the vacant Vassall house for his home and headquarters. Washington grew into his leadership role here as he plotted strategy with his military advisers and met with key figures such as John Adams, Benjamin Franklin, Benedict Arnold, and chiefs of Native American tribes. His wife Martha arrived in December with her son and daughter-in-law and her domestic staff. The couple celebrated their seventeenth wedding anniversary with a big party in the parlor. Once the Continental forces drove the British out of Boston in March 1776, Washington moved south to New York to prepare for the next series of battles.

Andrew Craigie, who had served as Apothecary General to the Continental Army, purchased the home in 1791. By then, Craigie was a freewheeling speculator in finance and real estate, capitalizing on his connections to gain insider knowledge. He and his wife Elizabeth renovated and expanded the house and threw such grand parties that it was soon known as "Castle Craigie." The couple's extravagant lifestyle plunged them into debt. Andrew died suddenly in 1819, before he was able to right his financial affairs. Elizabeth, who would live until 1841, was forced to take

in boarders to make ends meet. Henry Wadsworth Longfellow began renting two rooms in 1837.

Longfellow was something of an overachiever. He entered Bowdoin College in his native Maine at age 14 and was offered a three-year European study tour and a professorship upon graduation. When Harvard came calling a few years later, Longfellow, who spoke eight languages, returned to Europe with his wife Mary for another year of study. During their travels, Mary died of complications from a miscarriage. When Longfellow returned to Cambridge alone, he joined the Harvard faculty in the most prestigious professorship in the field now known as comparative literature.

Resuming his personal life did not come as easily. Before he returned from Europe, Longfellow had met Frances "Fanny" Appleton and her family in Switzerland. Her father was a founder of the Merrimac Manufacturing Company, which developed the mill system in Lowell and pioneered the American textile industry. When the Appletons returned from their grand tour, Longfellow was eager to court Fanny. Her father was skeptical of the poet-scholar, and Fanny, ten years younger than Longfellow, seemed little interested in his attentions. Even her family members were surprised when Fanny finally agreed to marry Longfellow in 1843. Nathan Appleton did give the couple the ultimate wedding gift—Castle Craigie.

The newlyweds were more thrilled with the home's link to history than to land speculator Craigie. Fanny wrote to her brother Thomas: "how noble an inheritance this is where Washington dwelt in every room." The couple had six children, five

of whom survived infancy. Fanny taught her children reading and geography and oversaw their religious education. She kept track of their young lives in her "Chronicles of the Children of Castle Craigie." Longfellow retired from teaching in 1854 to devote himself full-time to writing. Books like *Evangeline, The Song of Hiawatha,* and *Tales of a Wayside Inn* brought him widespread celebrity and made him the most popular writer of his day. The couple entertained frequently and welcomed everyone from Ralph Waldo Emerson and Charles Dickens to abolitionist Charles Sumner and the "Swedish Nightingale," Jenny Lind.

Tragedy struck in 1861. Fanny was sealing locks of the children's hair into envelopes when hot wax set her clothing on fire. Henry tried to smother the flames, but Fanny died the next day. Longfellow was so badly burned that he grew a full beard to cover the most obvious scars. As he mourned Fanny's death, he undertook a translation of Dante's *Divine Comedy,* channeling his grief into the author's journey through the three realms of the dead as he sought to recover his beloved Beatrice in the afterlife.

Tours of the house concentrate on the Longfellow years, touching on Henry's study, the large library where guests often gathered, and the private family quarters on the upper floor. Many visitors recognize the central stair from "The Children's Hour," Longfellow's loving evocation of his daughters "grave Alice, and laughing Allegra, and Edith with golden hair."

One of the last writers to visit Longfellow was the poet Oscar Wilde, during his 1882 lecture tour of America. Wilde recalled that "Longfellow himself was a beautiful poem." The gray eminence of American letters died in the house later that year and was buried in the family plot at Mount Auburn Cemetery (see page 168).

The house stayed in family hands. Although she traveled extensively, oldest daughter Alice lived her entire life in the home where she was born. Deeply committed to educational equality, she supported scholarships for Native American and African American students. In 1879, she helped found the Society for the Collegiate Instruction of Women, the forerunner of Radcliffe College. She hosted some early commencement ceremonies in the library.

Alice worked with landscape architects to restore the formal garden and added touches of her own, including a sundial at the center. Alice was behind the establishment of the Longfellow House Trust that opened the property to the public in 1930. (The Trust donated the property to the National Park Service in 1972.) Her nephew, Henry Wadsworth Longfellow "Harry" Dana, moved into the house in 1917 after Columbia University fired him for pacifist activities and socialist proclivities. The pair worked to archive all the objects in the house—socks, spoons, letters, journals, recipes for apple pie, and anything else they could find. Alice died in 1928, but Harry lived in the house until his death in 1950. Their efforts made the property one of the best-documented historic homes in America.

Mount Auburn Cemetery
580 Mount Auburn Street, Cambridge; 617-547-7105;
mountauburn.org; open year-round; check website for tours and
programs; free.

The graves of Mount Auburn Cemetery memorialize more than 95,000 people, yet the 175-acre graveyard brims with life. Founded in 1831, Mount Auburn was a progenitor of the garden cemetery movement in America. It marked a shift in attitudes toward death by evoking a vision of a peaceful afterlife amid nature's beauty. Even the word "cemetery" was a new coinage from Greek roots to denote an area where the dead repose.

Not all the impetus for creating Mount Auburn flowed from such ethereal concerns. In 1825, Dr. Jacob Bigelow, a physician and Harvard professor, assembled the region's civic leaders to address pressing health concerns of overcrowded urban burial grounds and new burials in congested neighborhoods. He proposed that they consider creating a large-scale burial ground. Père Lachaise, which had opened in 1804 at the edge of Paris, offered a model for a graveyard at a remove from residential districts.

In 1831, the founders voted to purchase a tract of rolling farmland near the Charles River that straddled the Cambridge-Watertown line. The property—which contained four ponds, seven small hills, several knolls and dells, and a mature forest of oak, beech, and pines—was selected, per the group's minutes, for its "rural beauty" and its "romantic seclusion."

The president of the new Massachusetts Horticultural Society, Henry A. S. Dearborn, undertook the design of the landscape, working with civil engineer Alexander Wardsworth. Although the cemetery has greatly expanded since its inception, the Dearborn-Wardsworth layout remains the primary template. Their winding carriage roads follow the land's contours. Wooded areas and ponds that reflect the flowering growth around their perimeters create a naturalistic landscape, capped by the striking view from the summit of Mount Auburn.

The beautiful garden landscape was intended to both console the bereaved and inspire visitors to contemplate their own mortality. As the first "rural" or garden cemetery in the United States, Mount Auburn helped establish the ideal of a cemetery as a tranquil retreat with flowers, grass, and trees. Bigelow was so enamored of the design that he predicted "in a few years ... no place in the environs of our city will possess stronger attractions to the visitor."

He was not wrong. In short order, Mount Auburn began to draw large numbers of visitors from around the United States and from abroad. Dearborn had modeled much of his design on English parks and estates, and the cemetery had a special resonance with British visitors. In 1860, the future King Edward VII—then the Prince of Wales—visited. Coverage in the local press gushed that he helped plant two trees "with his own royal hands." Despite its decorous associations, Mount Auburn welcomed all visitors, ultimately stoking a hunger for public green spaces and helping to launch America's park movement.

Cofounder Bigelow, who became the cemetery's second president, set the Romantic Picturesque tone for the built structures on the grounds. His Egyptian Revival Gateway design—the primary entrance gate—was first erected in 1832 as a wooden structure dusted with sand. When funds allowed, it was remade in Quincy

granite in 1842–1843. Bigelow modeled the gate on renderings of temples in the accounts of Napoleon's 1798–1801 expedition in Egypt. The stone version of his design, Bigelow said, would "entitle it to a stability of a thousand years."

Construction of the Gothic Revival chapel designed by Bigelow began in 1844. His neo-Norman watchtower on the summit of Mount Auburn, named in honor of George Washington, was finished a decade later. The 62-foot tower, designed with architect Gridley J. F. Bryant, emulates a common motif in English landscape design. Its medieval features, including Gothic windows and two levels of battlements, expressed the prevailing ideas of the picturesque.

More than 30,000 sculptural memorials fill the grounds, and they include major works by Augustus Saint-Gaudens, Thomas Crawford, and Edmonia Lewis, among others. To make the cemetery a place of inspiration, the founders encouraged the creation of monuments to civic heroes. One of the first was the obelisk erected to commemorate the members of the 1840 United States Naval Expedition who perished in the Fiji Islands. Bigelow commissioned a massive sphinx that sits atop the hill near the cemetery chapel. It marked the preservation of the Union in the Civil War and "the destruction of African slavery, by the uprising of a great people, by the blood of fallen heroes."

After the middle of the nineteenth century, the influences of John Ruskin and H. H. Richardson popularized Romanesque and Gothic architecture in Boston, a

trend reflected in the Gothic styling of sculptures and gravestones throughout the cemetery. Victorian sentimentalism also informed many of the grave sculptures of grieving women, guardian dogs, and—often on children's graves—sweet little lambs. Some of the plots were even fenced off and laid out like family parlors, with each member accorded her or his seat in the "room."

This extraordinary combination of park landscape and funerary art persists to the present. The original circulation system of the roadways has expanded—in part to permit the passage of automobiles—but the contours of the 1831 cemetery remain. Visitors still navigate by the nineteenth-century iron signs along roads and paths named for plants and trees. More than 5,000 trees of 600 varieties share the grounds with more than 250 species of shrubs and ground covers.

Winding paths and roads create changing vistas at every turn. The abundant blooming plants and considerable forest canopy attract vast numbers of migrating birds to this natural island in an urban landscape. MassAudubon has officially recognized the cemetery as one of the state's Important Bird Areas. More than 200 species are spotted here each year. At certain times of day, the binoculared birdwatcher is the dominant species on the grounds.

Some of the more than 200,000 yearly visitors seek out the illustrious dead, including poets Amy Lowell and Robert Creeley; inventor Edwin Land; hospital reformer Dorothea Dix; painter Winslow Homer; architects Charles Bulfinch, Benjamin Thompson, and Buckminster Fuller; authors Bernard Malamud and Henry Wadsworth Longfellow; civic leader Harrison Gray Otis; legendary preacher Phillips Brooks; poet and activist Julia Ward Howe; cookbook author Fannie Farmer; and even Mary Baker Eddy, founder of Christian Science. Contrary to urban legend, Eddy's tomb does not contain a telephone.

83

National Park Service
U.S. Department of the Interior

John Fitzgerald Kennedy
National Historic Site
Birthplace of America's 35th President

THE OUTER RING

John Fitzgerald Kennedy National Historic Site
83 Beals Street, Brookline; 617-566-7937; nps.gov/jofi; open for guided tours late May through October; free. T: Coolidge Corner

John Fitzgerald Kennedy once wrote that "There is within each man a very special affection for the place of his birth." For Kennedy, that place was the town of Brookline, where he spent his early formative years. More specifically, it was the second-floor bedroom of the house at 83 Beals Street where he was born on the afternoon of May 29, 1917.

Kennedy was the second child of Joseph P. Kennedy and Rose Fitzgerald Kennedy, both third-generation descendants of Irish immigrants. Their fathers had risen to prominent positions in Democratic politics. The couple embodied the story of Irish immigrants in Boston as they rose from economic refugees to brokers of political and economic power.

By the time the couple married in 1914, Joseph Kennedy had become one of the youngest bank presidents in the country. At that time, many young couples spent a few years living with their parents as they worked to establish themselves. But not the Kennedys. Fresh from their honeymoon, they moved into the three-story, nine-room Colonial Revival home on Beals Street. The house had been built about five years earlier in the streetcar suburb of Brookline. With a Catholic church, parks, and shops nearby, the neighborhood attracted many middle- and upper-middle-class Irish American families.

Three more Kennedy children were born in the house, and by 1920 the growing family moved to a larger house nearby. By 1927, they left Brookline for good. But the Beals Street home remained a touchstone. When the thirty-fifth president was assassinated in 1963, thousands of mourners gathered on the street outside.

In the years following Kennedy's death, the family repurchased the home as a memorial to the nation's first Irish Catholic president. For about three years, Rose Kennedy channeled her grief into returning the house to her family's early days.

"We were very happy here and although we did not know about the days ahead, we were enthusiastic and optimistic about the future," Mrs. Kennedy recalled in 1969, when the home was dedicated as a National Historic Site. Even with the gaps in her memory after so many years, the details of Mrs. Kennedy's remembrances paint a vivid picture of the joyful and busy days of her young family's life.

Mrs. Kennedy was even able to restore some of her family's furnishings to the house, particularly in the dining room. She considered that room to be the most important and the table is set with fine china and glassware that would be sure to impress guests. The couple's first two children, Joseph P. Kennedy Jr. and John Fitzgerald Kennedy, sat at a small table by a lace-curtained window. It is set with their silver spoons and porringers. Nearly two years older, Joe Jr. excelled at pleasing his parents while Jack sought attention by becoming the family clown. Their father encouraged competition between his sons and was determined that his children inherit his drive and ambition. As their children matured, Joe and Rose encouraged lively conversation and debate around the dining table.

Rose Kennedy did not consider the living room to be a formal space for adults only. She had fond memories of reading or sewing while her husband read the *Boston Transcript* and her children played in their pajamas before bedtime. The piano in the room was a wedding present from two of Rose's uncles. She had learned to play as a girl and studied piano at the New England Conservatory (see page 126). She had even accompanied her father, onetime Boston mayor John "Honey Fitz" Fitzgerald, on the piano when he sang at political rallies. In the evenings, the Kennedy family might gather around their piano to sing Irish songs and show tunes.

One of the upstairs bedrooms was used as a nursery, and displays include the crib and christening gown used by all nine children. (The last Kennedy to be christened in the gown was John F. Kennedy Jr.) A bookcase in the room reflects Rose's commitment to her children's education. Jack had been sickly as a child, and his mother had often read to him, fostering his lifelong love of reading. A small chair

in the room holds copies of the young boy's two favorite books, *King Arthur and the Knights of the Round Table* and *Billy Whiskers*, a tale of a mischievous little goat.

A small desk served as Mrs. Kennedy's command center to oversee the needs of the household. Two servants lived on the third floor and handled the cleaning, cooking, and basics of childcare. A third woman came in two days a week to do the laundry. That left Mrs. Kennedy free to concentrate on the proper upbringing of her children. To keep track of each child's growth and development, she kept note cards to record such things as illnesses and significant milestones. More importantly, she nurtured her children's curiosity and encouraged their interest in history and the arts. She sought to impart her own strong faith, often reminding them that "to whom much is given, much is expected."

Equipped with a Glenwood stove, wooden icebox, and soapstone sink, the kitchen on the first floor at the back of the house was the domain of the servants and left less of an impression on Mrs. Kennedy. She did recall, however, that the family ate Boston baked beans for dinner on Saturday nights—and then again for breakfast on Sunday mornings.

From such traditional New England beginnings, John Fitzgerald Kennedy was launched on a trajectory that would eventually lead to Pennsylvania Avenue.

Frederick Law Olmsted National Historic Site
99 Warren Street, Brookline; 617-566-1689; nps.gov/frla; grounds open daily year-round, visitor center April through December; free.

Frederick Law Olmsted was in his early sixties when he and his wife Mary moved from New York to Boston in 1883. The father of American landscape architecture had already established himself with his designs for such grand public spaces as Central Park in Manhattan, Prospect Park in Brooklyn, and South Park in Chicago. Very much a social reformer, Olmsted believed that all people needed fresh air and open spaces to soothe the body and lift the spirit. He was already in the process of creating the string of parks that would form Boston's Emerald Necklace.

Olmsted's choice to settle in the leafy suburb of Brookline was hardly random. As Americans were moving from the country to the city, Olmsted firmly believed that suburbs represented the future. People should live in the suburbs amid grass and trees, he argued, and commute via public transportation to downtown offices and factories. More specifically, Olmsted had his eye on a property on the corner of Warren and Dudley streets. Two elderly sisters lived in the 1810 house on the grounds. To persuade them to sell, Olmsted built the pair a cottage on an adjacent site where they could live rent-free.

As it turned out, Olmsted didn't actually commute to his job. By adding extensive office suites to the north side of the house, he essentially worked from home in the country's first full-scale professional landscape design practice. The property—which Olmsted dubbed Fairsted—was ideally suited for him to realize an abridged version of his design philosophy. The lot is essentially a bowl at the bottom of long inclines in all directions, but its undulating topography creates the illusion of much greater expanse than the approximately two-acre plot.

As if he were creating a large public park, Olmsted landscaped his property to create a series of distinctive environments and vistas that flow into one another to form a single, cohesive landscape. Ultimately, he installed more than 200 species (and uncounted numbers) of both woody and herbaceous plants in his quest for a landscape that, for all its Olmstedian intervention, would appear to be a happy accident of nature.

He began by defining the limits of his corner lot by planting Canadian and Carolina hemlocks at the boundary lines and erecting wooden fences just tall enough to screen out carriage traffic. Visitors enter Fairsted through a rustic spruce-pole gateway and proceed along a circular driveway toward the front door of the house. The drive surrounds a 30-foot-diameter mound inside a round curb of basalt and Roxbury puddingstone. The trees and shrubs planted on the mound help block views of the house from the road.

Stone steps lead from the driveway down to the Hollow, a sunken garden set in a natural depression at the northeast corner of the lot. Olmsted cloaked a series of terraces with shrubbery and laid out meandering paths lined with rhododendrons to create a cool retreat from the heat of summer. In fact, he carved a small cul-de-sac where he placed a desk so that he could work outdoors when it was warm.

In contrast to the Hollow, the Rock Garden at the southeast corner of the property occupies a rounded knoll. A path through a dense planting of shrubs, trees, and groundcovers plunges into an unusually dense and lush woodland. The path leads upward to a rock garden of mosses and low groundcovers. Visitors who walk the path in a clockwise direction feel as if they are stepping from the woods into a broad and bright meadow. This dramatic view of the South Lawn is perhaps the most unexpected vista on the Fairsted grounds.

When Olmsted purchased the property, the South Lawn was covered in trees. He saved only a single American Elm at the center. It survived until 2011 and was replaced with a more disease-resistant variety two years later. So he could enjoy the view of the South Lawn, Olmsted constructed an enclosed porch on the residential side of the house. From there he could gaze across the grassy lawn to a stand of tall Canadian hemlocks flanked by rhododendrons and scarlet firethorn bushes—a view that evokes the edge of a dense New England woods. To the left of this stand, Olmsted planted lush but low ostrich ferns to lead the eye out of his landscape and into one of his favorite "borrowed views," the long stretch of meadow on the adjoining property.

The Biltmore Estate in Asheville, North Carolina, was Olmsted's last major project before he retired in 1895. His sons Frederick Law Olmsted Jr. and John Charles Olmsted continued operating the design firm and enlarged the offices as the business grew. Mary lived in the house until her death in 1921. Over the next five decades, various tenants used the living quarters while the design firm remained in the offices.

The property was designated as a National Historic Landmark in 1963. Sixteen years later Congress authorized the purchase of the property and archives by the National Park Service, which began a process of restoration. The property's appearance has been rolled back to roughly 1920, when it still contained all of Frederick Law Olmsted's major design strokes with some modifications by his sons. The Olmsted Archives at Fairsted contain more than a million original documents. They chronicle more than 6,000 landscape design projects—from public parks to college campuses, zoos, railway stations, and private estates—that the Olmsted firm executed between the 1850s and 1979.

But no Olmsted vista is quite as personal as the grounds at Fairsted that the master created for his own pleasure and delight.

Arnold Arboretum
Hunnewell Visitor Center, 125 Arborway; 617-524-1718;
arboretum.harvard.edu; visitor center and grounds open year-round,
check website for schedule of free guided tours. T: Forest Hills

City dwellers need a place where they can mark the seasons through changes in a
living landscape—a place to welcome the hopeful beginnings of spring with pussy
willows and bright yellow forsythia, to inhale the sweet scent of lilacs as summer
approaches, and to greet autumn with the blazing red foliage of maples. In Boston,
that place is the Arnold Arboretum, the first public arboretum in North America
and model for many around the world.

The arboretum was established in 1872 with a bequest to Harvard University
from the estate of James Arnold. A New Bedford whaling merchant, Arnold was
also an amateur horticulturist known for inviting the public to visit his own gardens.
His gift was intended to create a tree farm that would "contain, as far as practicable,
all the trees [and] shrubs ... either indigenous or exotic, which can be raised in the
open air." In practice, of course, that means primarily trees and shrubs of the North
Temperate Zone that can withstand harsh New England winters.

Harvard first set aside 137 acres of its Bussey estate (also a bequest) in the Boston neighborhood of Jamaica Plain. The arboretum has since grown to 281 acres with
17,105 plants representing 3,846 taxa. Twelve percent of the plant species—more

than 1,000 individual specimens—are now threatened with extinction in the wild. In a very real sense, the arboretum collection functions as a biological ark. Under the terms of a 1,000-year lease, the arboretum is owned by the city of Boston and managed by Harvard. The unique partnership seems to work equally well for scientists and for folks just seeking a peaceful escape from city life.

Charles Sprague Sargent, a Harvard graduate in biology, was appointed as the first director of the Arnold Arboretum in 1873 and oversaw its growth and development until his death in 1927. One of Sprague's early decisions shaped the face of the arboretum and dictated the lyrical as well as scientific arrangement of the property. In 1877 he commissioned pioneering landscape architect Frederick Law Olmsted (see page 180) to design the grounds.

Olmsted pronounced the site suitable for "the best arboretum in the world." It was a challenge that he clearly relished because it coincided neatly with his own theories about the importance of natural spaces for the health of the city and its residents. "We want a ground to which people may easily go, where they shall, in effect, find the city put far away from them," Olmsted wrote. "We want depth of wood enough about it not only for comfort in hot weather, but to completely shut out the city from our landscapes."

The arboretum became one of the natural landscapes in Olmsted's Emerald Necklace that stretches seven miles through the city from Boston Common and the Public Garden (see pages 1 and 89) to Franklin Park. For the Bussey property, Olmsted devised several artificial ponds and a network of winding roads and pathways that follow the natural contours of the land with its brooks, meadows, and forest. The Arnold Arboretum is the only surviving arboretum designed by Olmsted and is considered one of the landscapes that remains most true to his vision.

Tree planting began in 1885, with naturalistic groupings of trees and shrubs by family and genus. Plant material flowed in from all over the world. The arboretum also mounted its own collecting efforts, most famously the early twentieth-century expeditions under Ernest H. Wilson in western China. The arboretum calls itself a "living museum" and continues to add to its collection, which emphasizes temperate woody species from North America and eastern Asia. The grounds are particularly rich in beech, honeysuckle, crab apple, oak, rhododendron, and lilac.

All that leafy beauty is also a living laboratory for plant science. Research projects at the arboretum have included studying the evolution of the relationships among species using molecular genetics and the fine-tuning of our understanding of plant physiology and morphology. Caring for the collection has led to advancements in propagation of woody plants, understanding of plant diseases and other pathologies, and ways to use integrated pest management to reduce the use of chemical pesticides.

But the rigors of research are far from the minds of the joggers, dog-walkers, and stroller-pushers who relish this woodsy paradise in the heart of the city. Most enter through the main gate from the Arborway and often stop first at the Hunnewell Visitor Center to check out the exhibitions and perhaps pick up a map.

Against a backdrop of rich green, the arboretum unfolds in a riot of color and scent from early spring through fall, with daffodils bursting into bloom in April and cherry, crab apple, and other fruit trees coming to life in early May. Mostly clustered around Bussey Hill Road, the arboretum's roughly 400 lilac plants of 180 species

constitute one of the top collections in North America and guarantee a joyful, fragrant series of blooms for about five weeks. Since the early twentieth century, Bostonians have eagerly awaited Lilac Sunday, a one-day celebration complete with tours, family activities, and the rare privilege of enjoying a usually prohibited picnic.

The blooms just keep coming with dogwoods and magnolias, azaleas and rhododendrons, hydrangeas and hibiscus. One five-acre garden is devoted to plants in the rose family, including a metal arbor that supports delicate white tea roses and blush pink hedgerow roses. In contrast to this orderly cultivation, the Cosmopolitan Meadow on Weld Hill is planted with a wildflower mix developed by an arboretum research scientist to bloom throughout the growing season.

Although species are often bunched together, and most plants carry a small metal ID tag, the layout of the Arnold Arboretum is more broadly ecological than descriptive or even ornamental. Sargent envisioned that "a visitor driving through the Arboretum will be able to obtain a general idea of the arborescent vegetation of the north temperate zone without even leaving his carriage."

Plantings flow one into another, and species are interplanted to provide a more natural environment—both for the birds and insects and for the people who come to appreciate the displays. While the plantings might help homeowners visualize how a specific shrub or tree might look on their own properties, the sheer natural beauty often undermines such rational intentions in favor of immersion in the landscapes of scent, color, and form.

Olmsted was right. The urban world does seem very far removed from this tranquil spot. But those who seek a reminder need only climb to the summit of 240-foot Peters Hill or 198-foot Bussey Hill for a view of the distant Boston city skyline peeking through the leafy canopy.

Shirley-Eustis House
33 Shirley Street, Roxbury (Boston); 617-442-2275; shirleyeustishouse.org; open for tours June through September; admission charged.

If it is true that history is written by the victors, it is no surprise that Boston has so many sites that recount the lives and times of the patriots of the American Revolution and so few that recall the representatives of British power in Boston. Among the most notable exceptions, the Old State House (see page 19) was the seat of British rule, while the Shirley-Eustis House presents a rare look at the more personal life of a royal governor in the decades before the Revolution.

William Shirley served as Royal Governor of the Province of Massachusetts Bay from 1741 to 1749 and again from 1753 to 1756. These days, his imposing Georgian mansion seems to have been dropped into a dense Boston neighborhood. But Roxbury was still bucolic farmland when Shirley selected the area for his country estate. Built in 1747, the two-and-a-half-story home rose above a stone basement and was topped by a cupola. Sited on a hill, it was visible from Boston Harbor. The grandest house in Roxbury was fitting for someone who was addressed as "your excellency." One of only four royal colonial governor's mansions still standing in the United States, the house is the only one expressly built by a governor.

Shirley may have been able to escape downtown Boston during the heat of summer, but he was not able to evade his royal duties. He and his wife Frances often hosted receptions and state banquets in their Roxbury home. Shirley was the representative of King George II in Boston, so even his getaway house had to reflect his status. Giant pilasters on the facade gave the home a stately mien. A double flight of stone steps made for a dramatic entrance into a large hall with a blue and white checked marble floor and an elegant staircase.

The hall leads into a two-story-high salon that had a musician's gallery over the entrance during Shirley's time. But the room's most dramatic feature is a giant Palladian window that offered a distant view of Boston Harbor. (Shirley would climb to the cupola when he wanted to check on ships in the harbor.) It is easy to imagine the room full of music and conversation and people in their finery. If the salon represents Shirley's public face, his small studio, also on the main level, was his private sanctuary and held his cabinet of curiosities. Still very much a British gentleman, Shirley would retreat into this space to sit at his desk and ponder the prints, drawings, maps, and books that he had gathered around him.

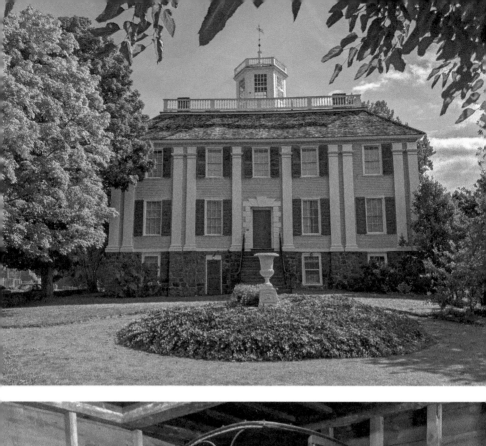

Shirley served as Governor of the Bahamas during the 1760s before returning to Boston. He died in his Roxbury home in 1771 and was interred at King's Chapel Burying Ground (see page 10). His home was confiscated during the Revolutionary War and served as a hospital and as barracks for the Massachusetts Sixth Regiment during the Siege of Boston.

A succession of wealthy merchants occupied the mansion after the war, and they began to remodel Shirley's estate in the Federal style favored during the early years of the Republic. That transformation was completed after the mansion was purchased by Dr. William Eustis in 1819. Eustis served as a surgeon during the Revolutionary War and was soon drawn into politics. He was elected to the state legislature and later to the United States House of Representatives before being appointed as Minister to the Netherlands in 1814. He purchased the Shirley house on his return from Europe, writing to a friend that it would be "the last extravagant act of my life."

Eustis had the musician's gallery in the salon dismantled and filled the volume of the space with a dramatic stairway. He was elected governor of Massachusetts while living in the house and also continued to see patients. Now named for the two very different governors, the mansion reflects the tastes and ambitions of both a representative of the British empire and a mover and shaker of the new Republic.

Following her husband's death in 1825, Caroline Eustis remained in the house until her own death in 1865. As her fortunes declined, she rented the lower level to a local farmer. From her cozy bedroom on the front of the house she could look out on

her elaborate gardens and fruit trees. During her widowhood, Roxbury blossomed as Boston's garden community, and Caroline Eustis was one of the few women to display her flowers under her own name at exhibitions of the Massachusetts Horticultural Society. She is also known to have exhibited Bartlett pears, perhaps influenced by neighbor Enoch Bartlett, who developed the variety. Today's gardens hint at the landscaping under both the Shirley and Eustis families without directly replicating either era.

The house was sold several years after Caroline Eustis's death. The logistics are hard to imagine, but it was actually moved about 60 feet to the southwest to make way for a new street pattern. By the early twentieth century, the former mansion had been divided into tenement housing for twenty families. Fortunately it was saved from demolition and finally fully restored in the 1980s. Some furnishings date to Shirley's time, but the home most fully represents the wealthy, European-influenced taste of the Eustis family.

Like William and Francis Shirley, William and Caroline Eustis were known for their hospitality. George Washington did visit, though he never slept here. A carriage house moved to the property in 1999 holds a Eustis family coach. It is believed that Governor Eustis sent the coach to the Rhode Island border in 1824 so that the Marquis de Lafayette could complete his journey to Boston in style. Lafayette came to town to dedicate the Bunker Hill Monument (see page 85) and he *did* spend the night at the Eustis estate.

Brook Farm
670 Baker Street, West Roxbury (Boston); 617-698-1802; mass .gov/locations/brook-farm-historic-site; open year-round; free.

When the United States was still in its infancy, it seemed a place of infinite possibility—and fertile ground for fledgling utopian social experiments. Brook Farm was among the idealistic attempts at communal living that sprang up in the first half of the nineteenth century. It only lasted for six years and was hardly the largest of such social experiments. Yet Brook Farm's association with some of the country's most influential thinkers and writers has secured its place in American social and philosophical history.

Former Unitarian minister George Ripley and his wife Sophia founded the Brook Farm Institute for Agriculture and Education in 1841. They were members of the Transcendental Club, a group of idealistic thinkers and intellectuals that coalesced around Ralph Waldo Emerson in Concord. The Club members, including Henry David Thoreau, Nathaniel Hawthorne, and Margaret Fuller, drew their inspiration from Emerson's book *Nature*, published in 1836. Members held often very different views on how their ideas should be implemented. Following Emerson's line of thinking, however, they did agree that making life on earth better was preferred to counting on pie in the sky when you die.

The Ripleys decided to put their philosophical principles into practice on a 192-acre former dairy farm in West Roxbury, then a farming community separate from Boston. They hoped to create a self-sufficient community and required each member to buy at least one share for $500. From about twenty members at its inception, Brook Farm grew to about 120 members at its peak. In addition to intellectuals and teachers, the community attracted carpenters, printers, shoemakers, and others with practical skills.

Nathaniel Hawthorne was one of the original shareholders. In fact, he was so convinced that living a simple life among like-minded people would nurture his writing that he purchased two shares. In an 1841 letter, Hawthorne wrote that "This is one of the most beautiful places I ever saw in my life. . . . There are woods, in which we can ramble all day."

In keeping with its egalitarian premises, Brook Farm required all members to work, although there was quite a bit of leeway in allowing each member to choose exactly which aspect of the workload to shoulder. When the day's work was done, the community might gather for intellectual discussions. They also found time for music, dancing, playing card games or charades, putting on plays, and holding costume parties. They went sledding and ice-skating in the winter and enjoyed picnics in the summer.

Brook Farm also endeavored to play a role in the social and political discourse of its age, publishing a weekly magazine called *The Harbinger*. Thinkers outside the Brook Farm community also contributed to the magazine. Among them were Horace Greeley, founder of the fledgling *New-York Tribune*; poet and abolitionist firebrand John Greenleaf Whittier; and poet James Russell Lowell, who would become the first editor of *The Atlantic Monthly*.

Although the stony soil was ill-suited to row crops, the farm managed to be self-supporting through growing grains and tree fruits. Brook Farm also relied heavily on tuition from students outside the community who attended its schools. As a self-consciously intellectual experiment in the perfectability of humankind, Brook Farm was committed to nurturing the life of the mind from nursery school through preparation for college. Classroom hours were flexible as students also participated in the never-ending work of tending a farm and ensuring the smooth operation of a large socialist community. The distribution of work, however, had not evolved to the point of sexual egalitarianism. (That would be left to a later generation of socialist thinkers.) The boys worked in the fields while the girls handled kitchen chores and laundry.

As the community expanded, the original farmhouse, called the Hive, and the school building were augmented with more houses, workrooms, and dormitories. But disaster struck in March 1846 when an ambitious new building was destroyed by fire shortly before it was completed. Finances were already shaky, and Brook Farm was unable to bounce back.

It did not help the community's precarious situation that Nathaniel Hawthorne had sued to try to recover his $1,000 investment. Finding the realities of farmwork utterly incompatible with his writing life, Hawthorne had decamped from Brook Farm after only six months. He made the best of the experience, however, using his time there as research for his 1852 novel *The Blithedale Romance*. Considered one of Hawthorne's most bitterly satirical works, the book paints an unflattering picture of life in a utopian community.

The group disbanded in 1847 and Ripley went on to work for Horace Greeley as the literary critic for the *New-York Tribune*. The land was turned to other uses, including as a poor farm for the town of West Roxbury. In 1861, the Second Massachusetts Infantry Regiment trained here before facing fire at Gettysburg, Atlanta, and other Civil War battlegrounds.

After a brief stint as a summer boardinghouse, Brook Farm became the property of the Lutheran Services Association, which operated a home for orphans from 1872 to 1943, and a residential treatment center and school from 1948 to 1974. The Lutherans also established Gethsemane Cemetery in 1873 and built the Print Shop in the late nineteenth century. The tall, two-story wooden structure still stands.

Brook Farm was designated as a National Historic Landmark in 1965. Since then, two properties most associated with the utopian community have been destroyed by fire. The Hive, the farmhouse occupied by George and Sophia Ripley and the original members of their grand experiment, burned in 1977. Seven years later, fire took the Margaret Fuller Cottage, which had been constructed around 1842 in the shape of a Maltese cross. The writer and advocate for women's rights took an active interest in Brook Farm, but never actually stayed in the cottage.

The walking map on the website of the Massachusetts Department of Conservation & Recreation, current owners of the property, marks the sites of the Hive and the Fuller Cottage. But somehow it seems appropriate that this property associated with Transcendentalists and their adoration of Nature has largely returned to its natural state of fields, wetlands, and woodlands with the Sawmill Brook running through it. Perhaps Hawthorne's first instinct was right. Brook Farm proved less an ideal utopian community than acres of lovely woods where a visitor can follow his lead and "ramble all day."

THEMATIC INDEX

ACKNOWLEDGMENTS

We would like to thank editor Amy Lyons for her enthusiasm for this project and the staff at the Globe Pequot Press for wrestling our manuscript into the book you have in your hands.

When we began this project, we had no idea that within weeks we would be engulfed in the lockdowns and closures of the COVID-19 pandemic. Yet time and again the staff and volunteers associated with Boston's National Historic Landmarks stepped forward to assist us with our research. Some of them even let us in the doors so we could refresh our memories and document properties in photographs. Quite literally, this book would not have been possible without them.

Finally, we are indebted to the readers of *Historic New England*, our preceding book about the region's National Historic Landmarks, as well as to those who turned out to our readings and talks, often arranged by local librarians. Your enthusiasm was so contagious that we were encouraged to write this follow-up title. Thank you, one and all!

ABOUT THE AUTHORS

Patricia Harris and David Lyon are frequent contributors to the *Boston Globe* and authors of more than thirty books on travel, food, and art. Their most recent title is *Historic New England: A Tour of the Region's Top 100 National Landmarks*, also published by Globe Pequot. This volume continues the exploration of places and people who have helped shape the region. Harris and Lyon live in Cambridge, Massachusetts, within walking distance of Harvard Yard. They make their online home at HungryTravelers.com.